The Amazing
Table Coasters
Coloring Book

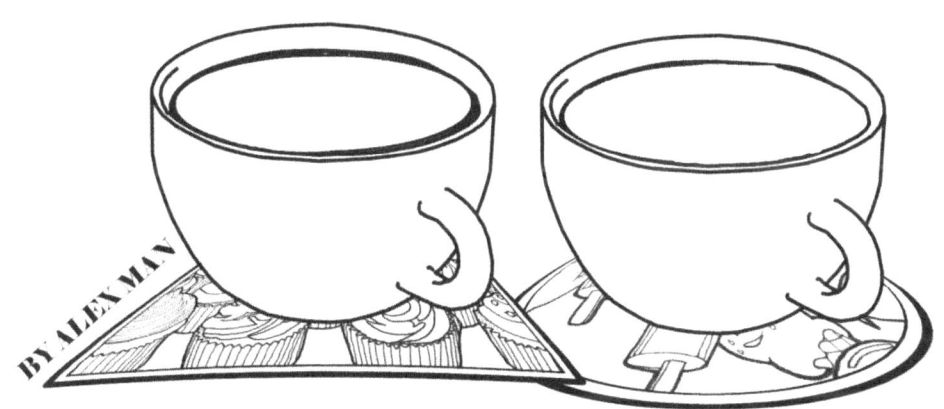

INSTRUCTIONS:
COLOR AND CUT THE COASTERS.

TIP:
FOR THE COASTERS TO LAST,
LAMINATE OR PASTE THEM ONTO A CARDBOARD.

Table of Contents:

Animals_____

New- York_____

Cupcake_____

Donuts_____

Ice Cream_____

Pizza_____

Eggs_____

Bread_____

Pretzel_____

Burger_____

Fruits_____

Veggies_____

Taekwondo_____

Flowers_____

Empty frames_____

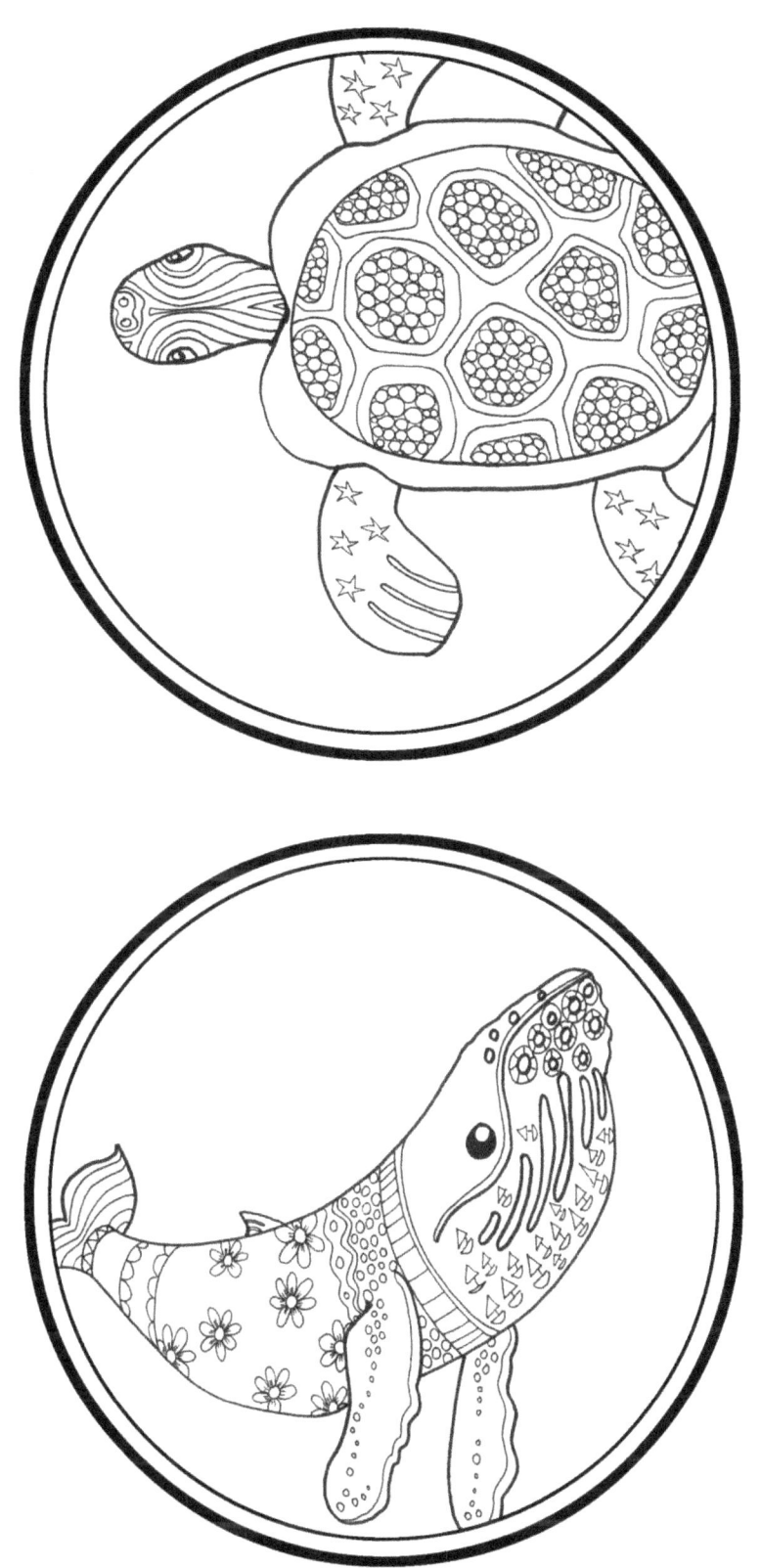

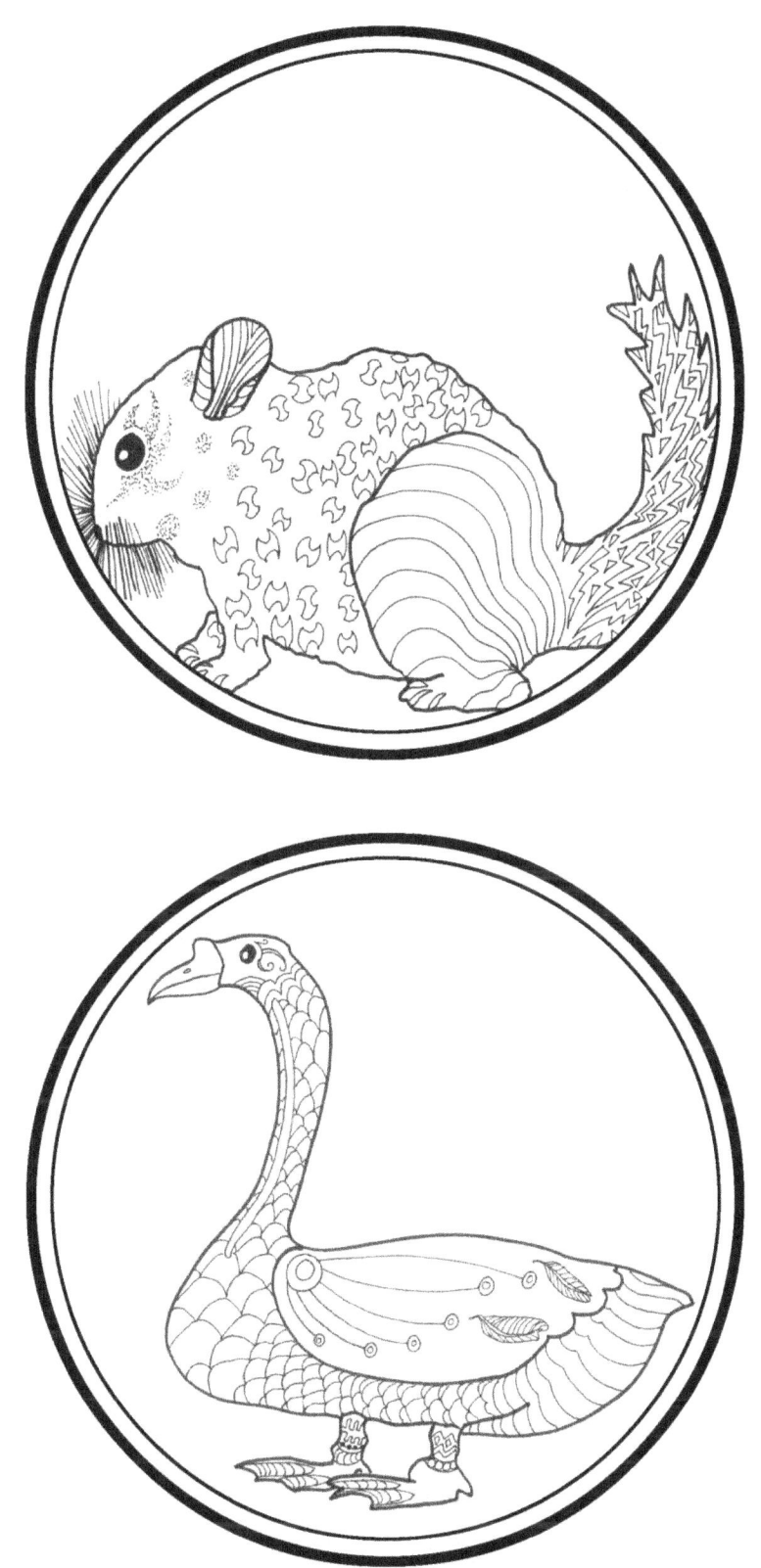

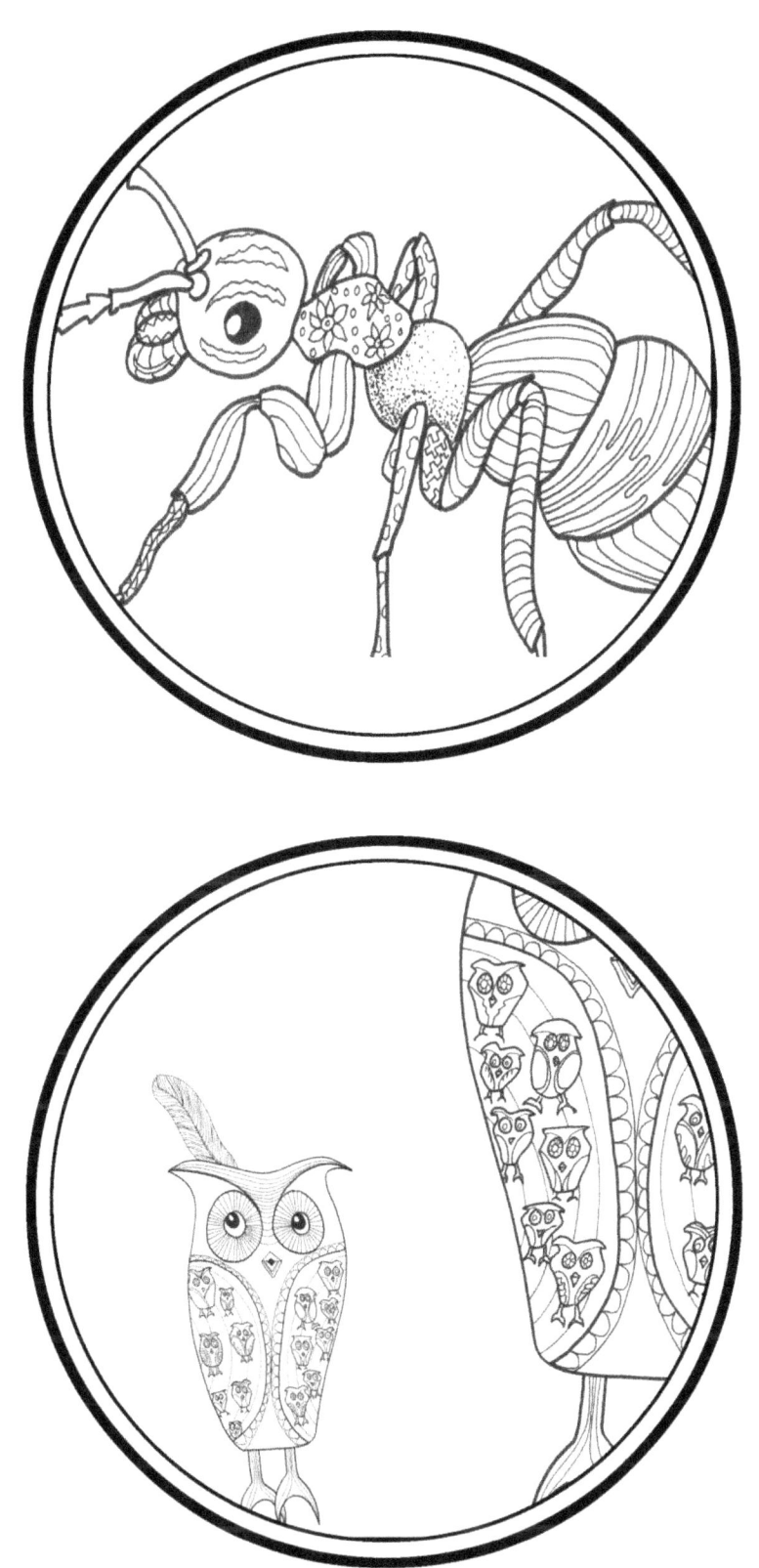

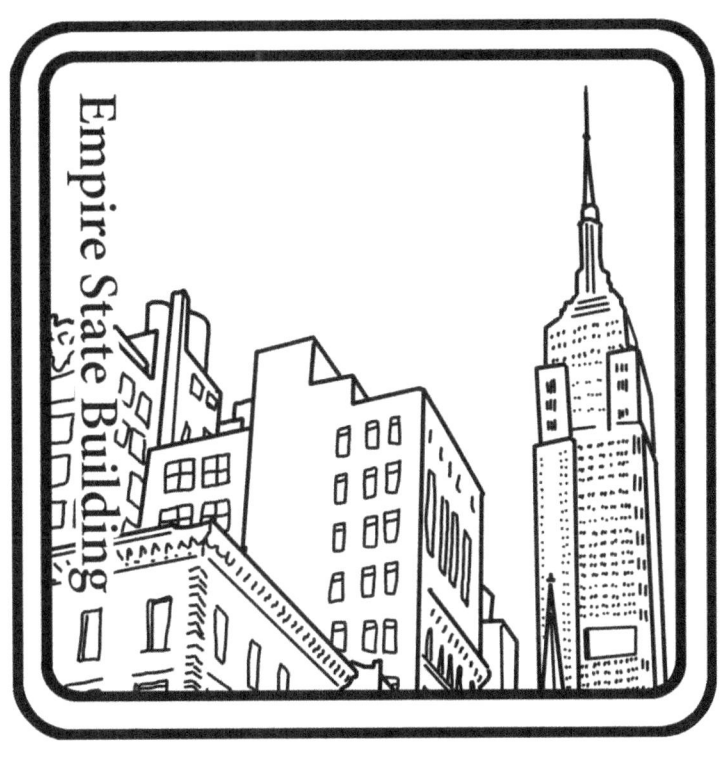

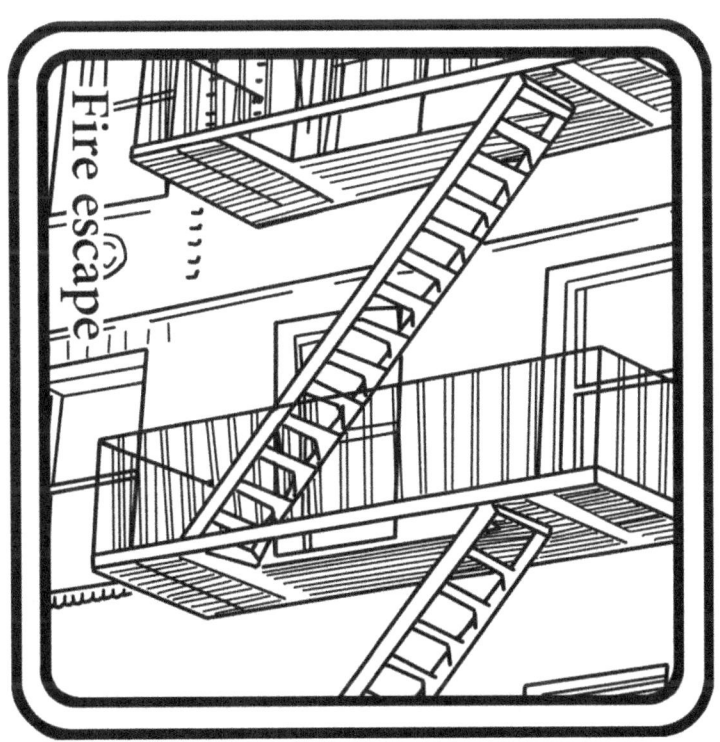

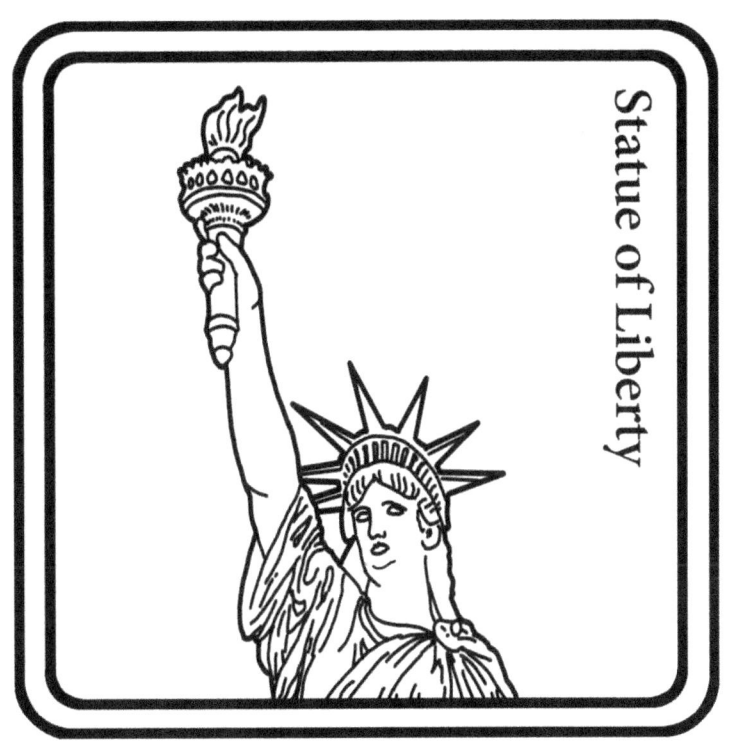

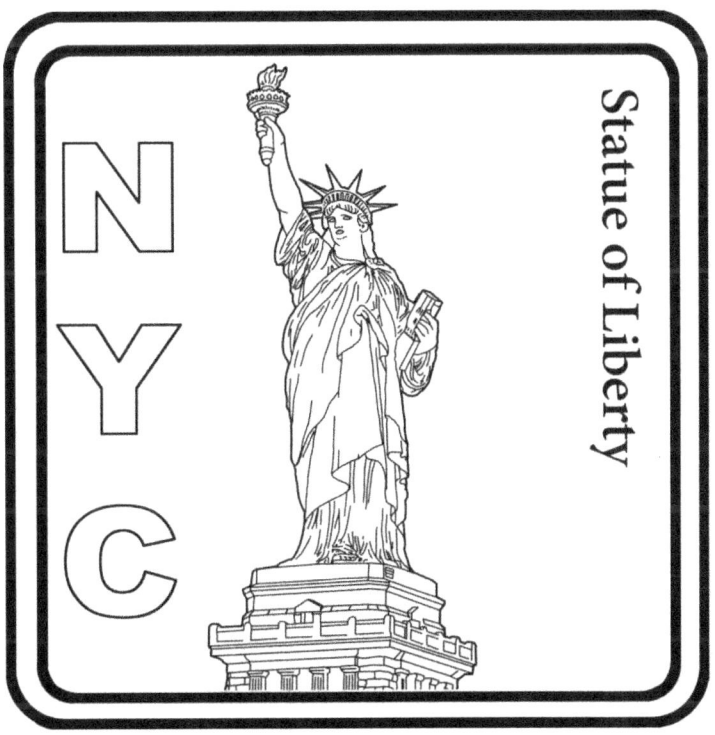

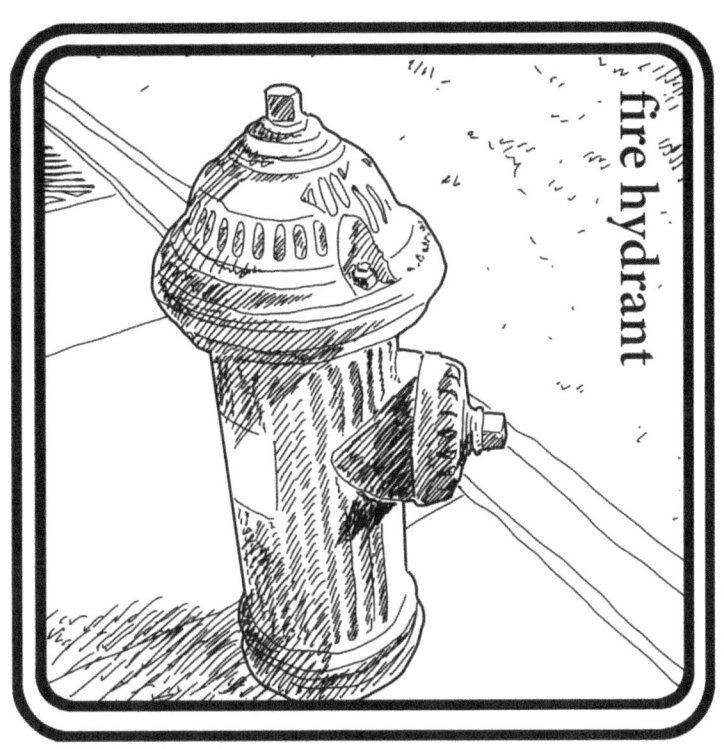
fire hydrant

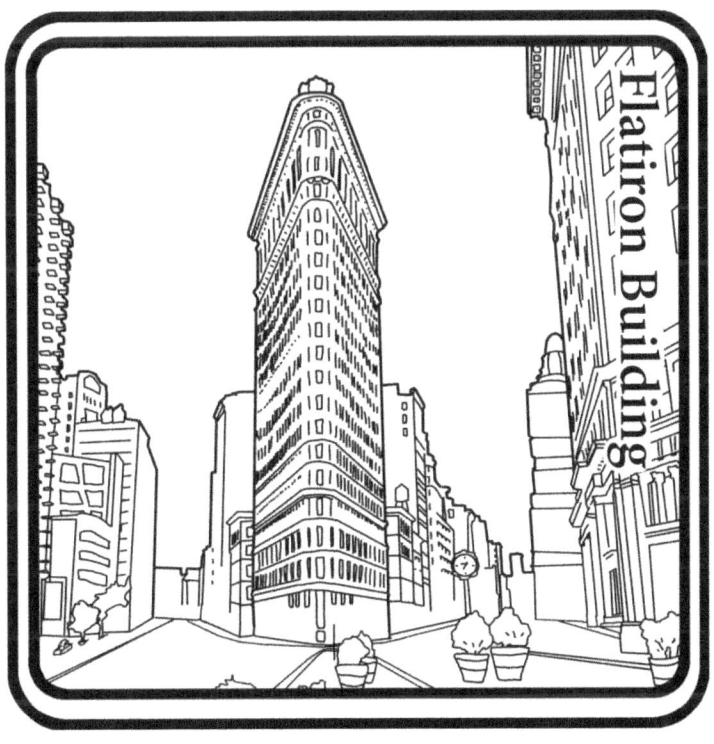
Flatiron Building

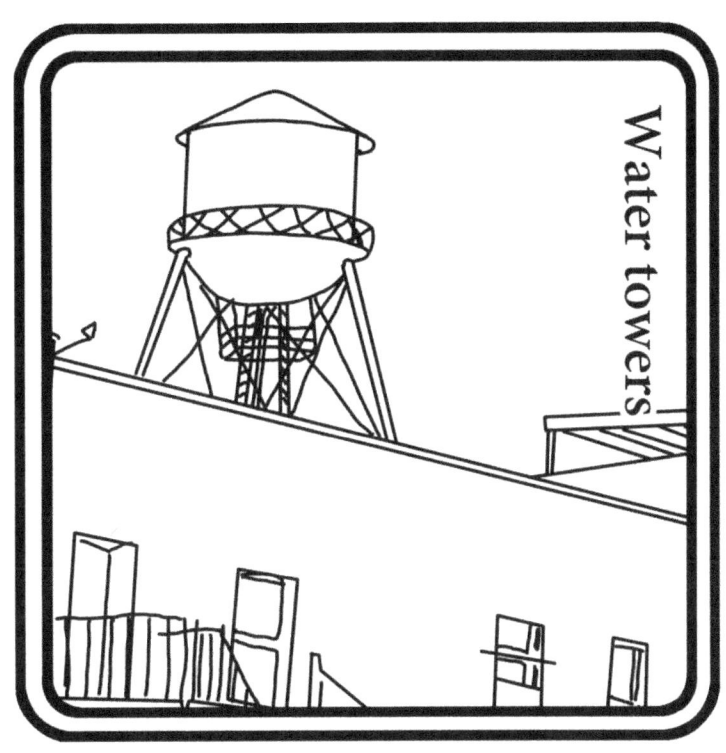
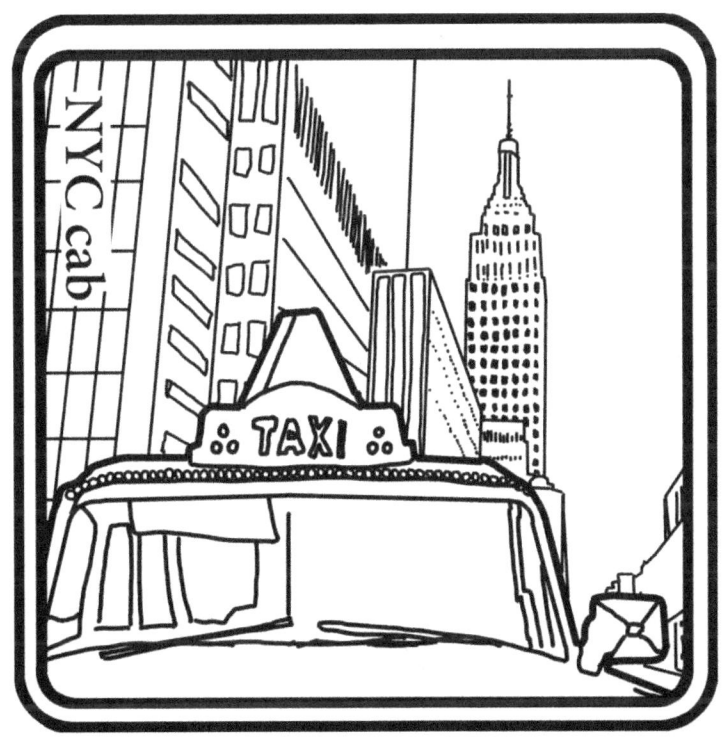

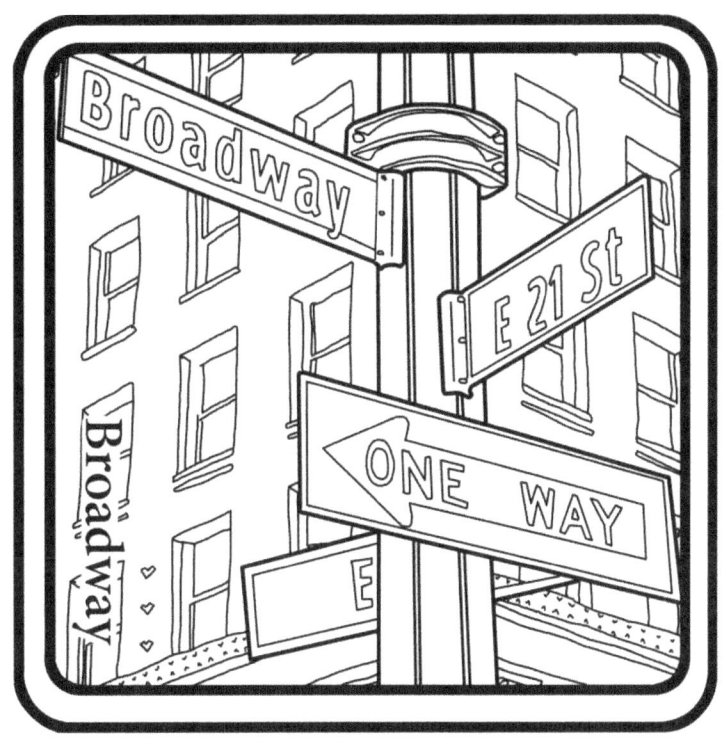

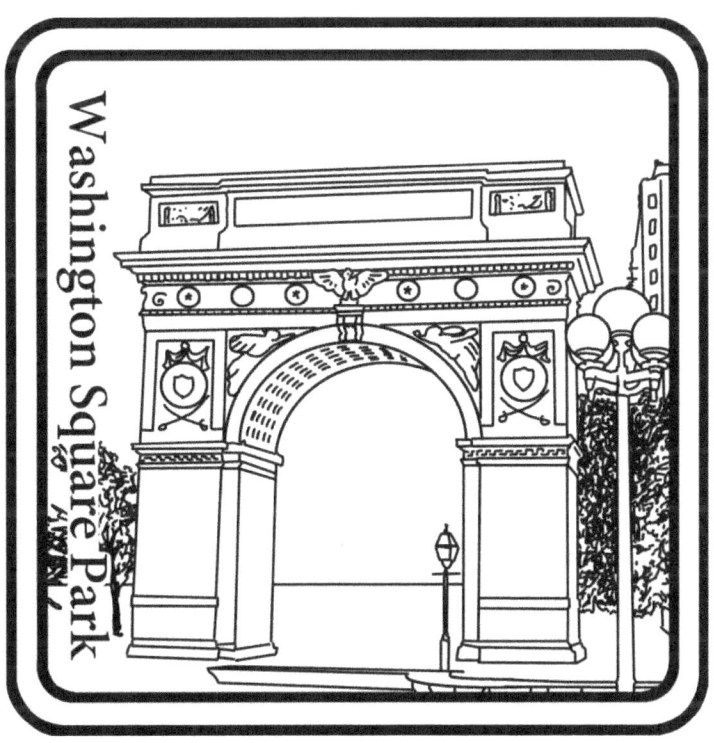

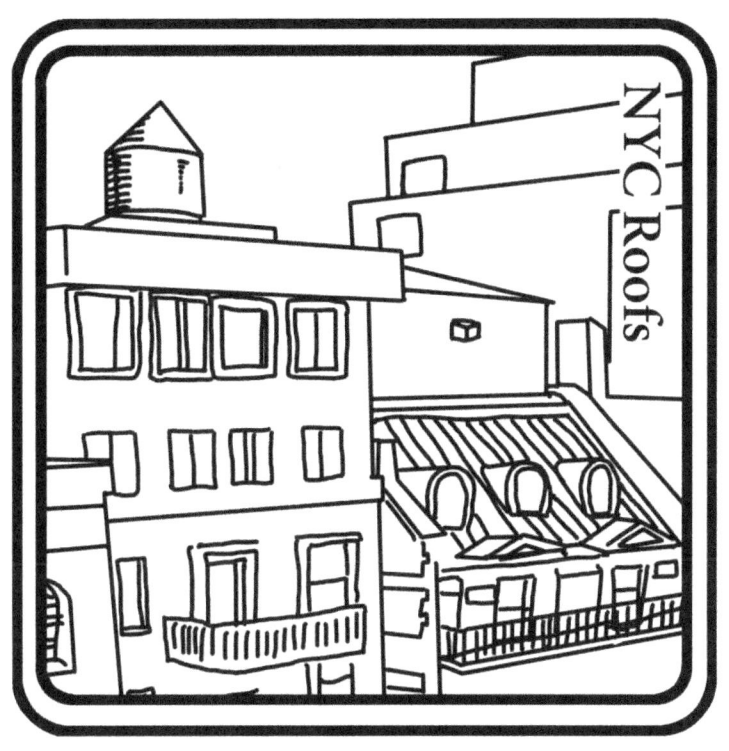
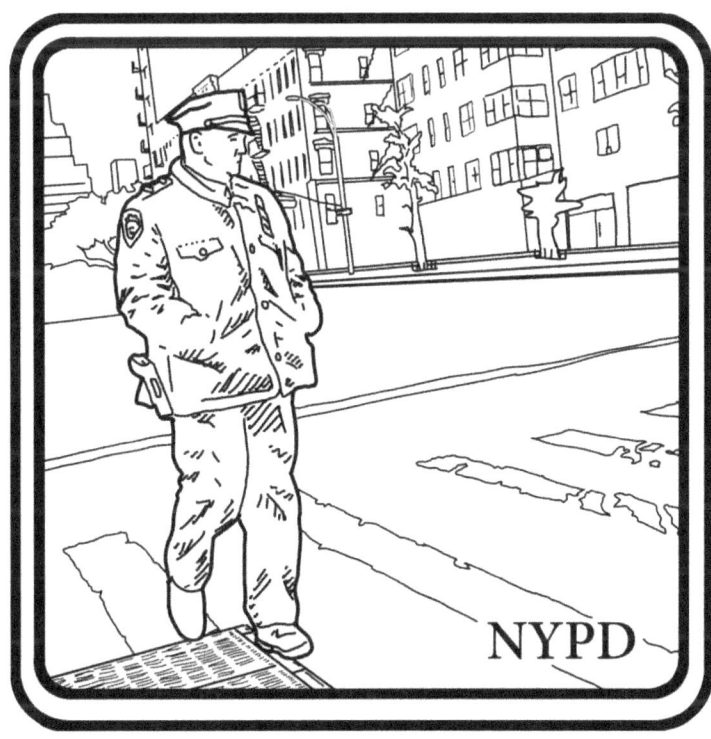

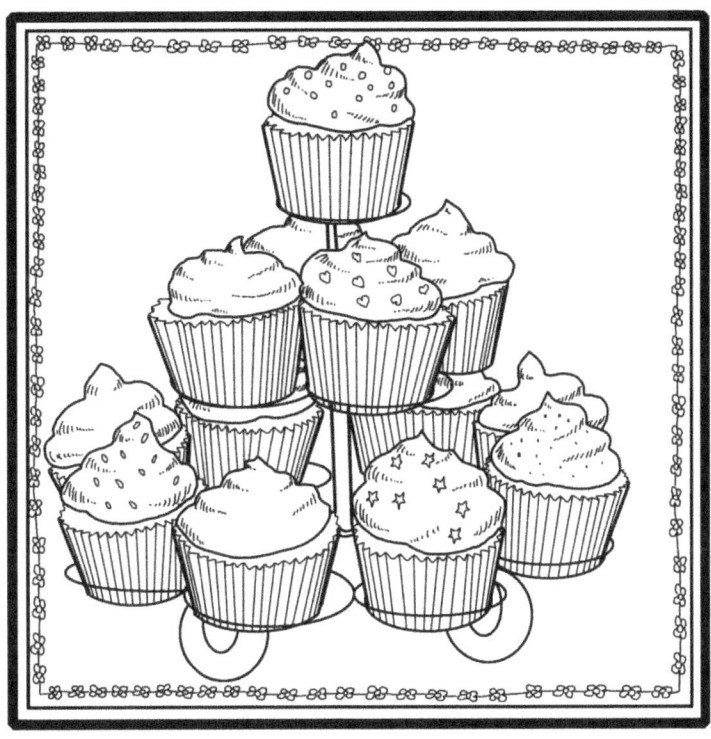
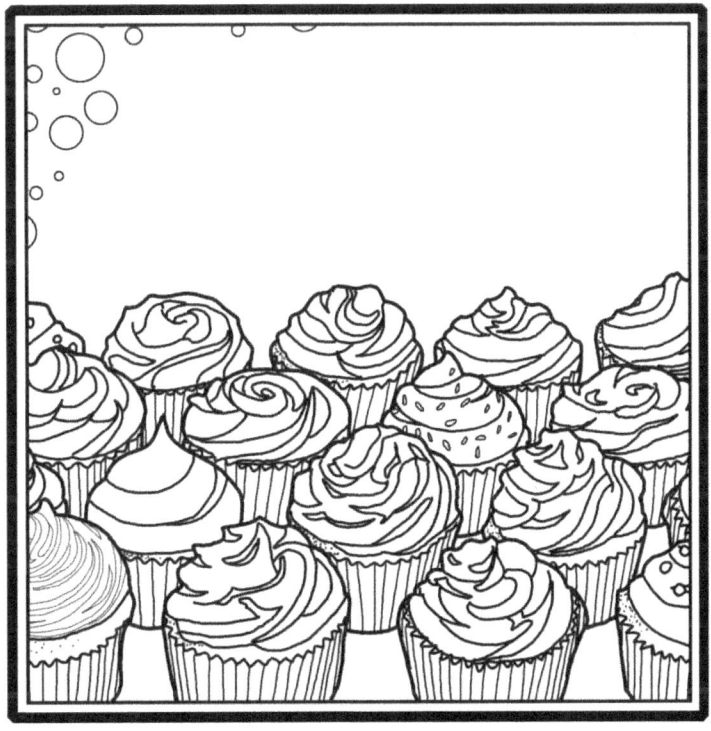

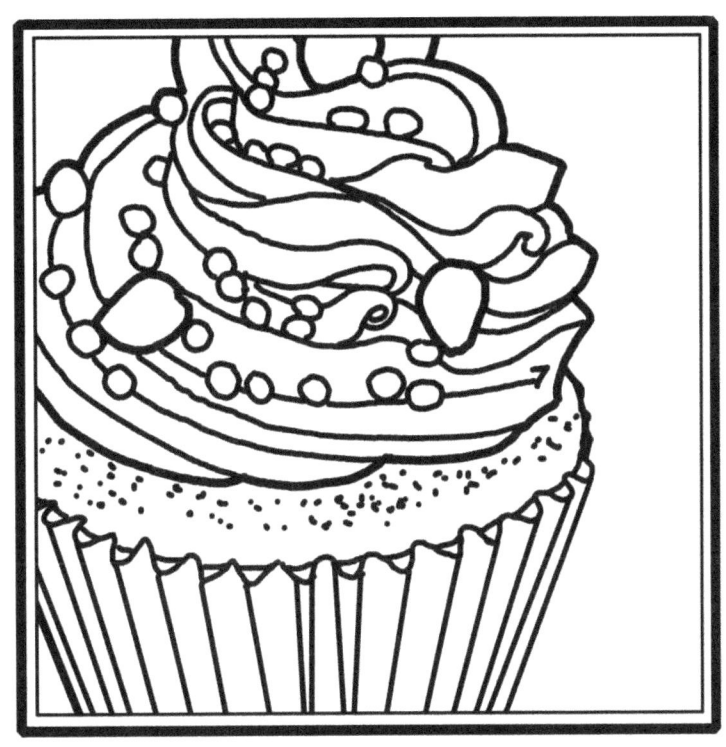
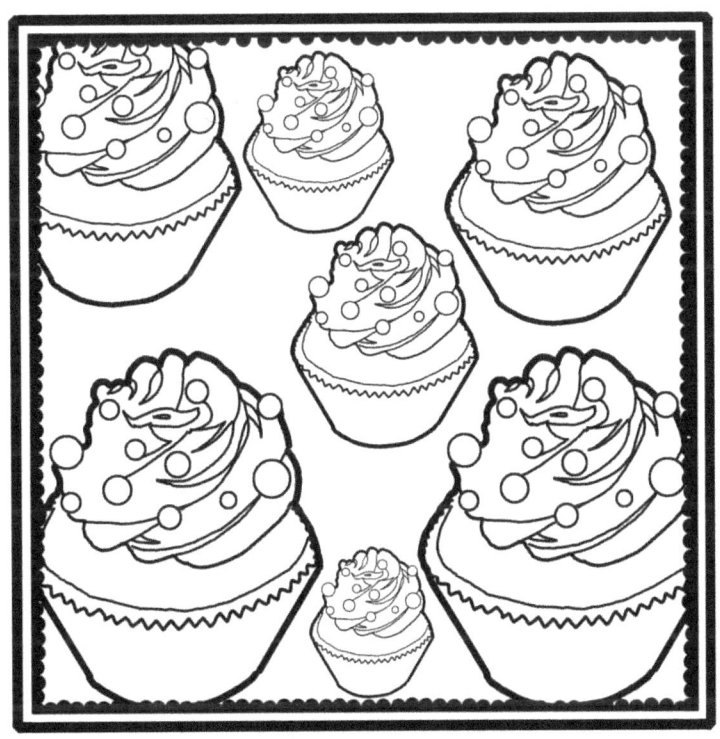

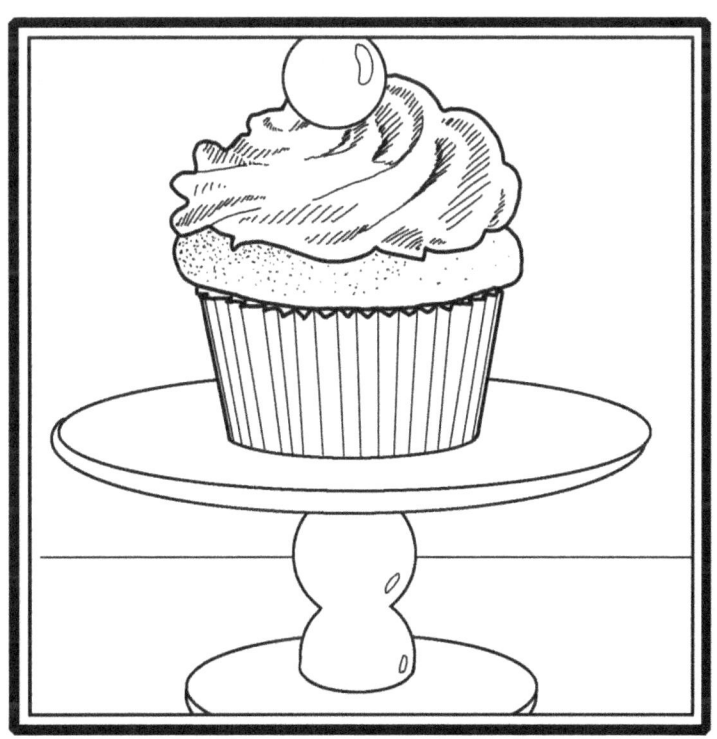

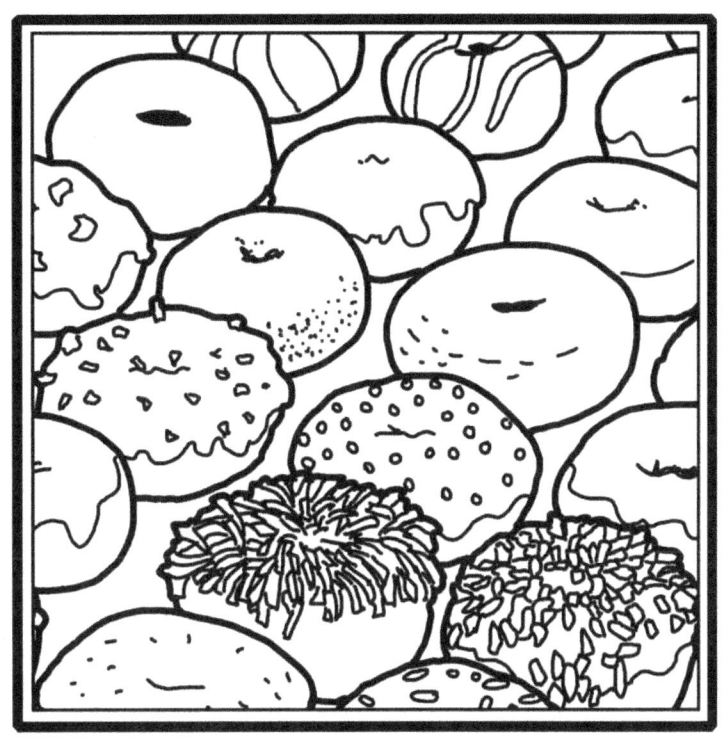

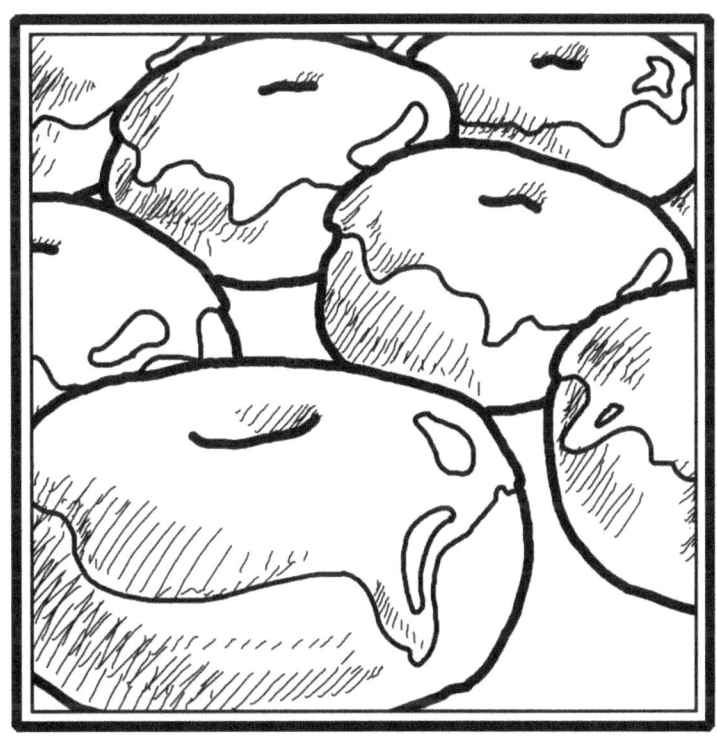

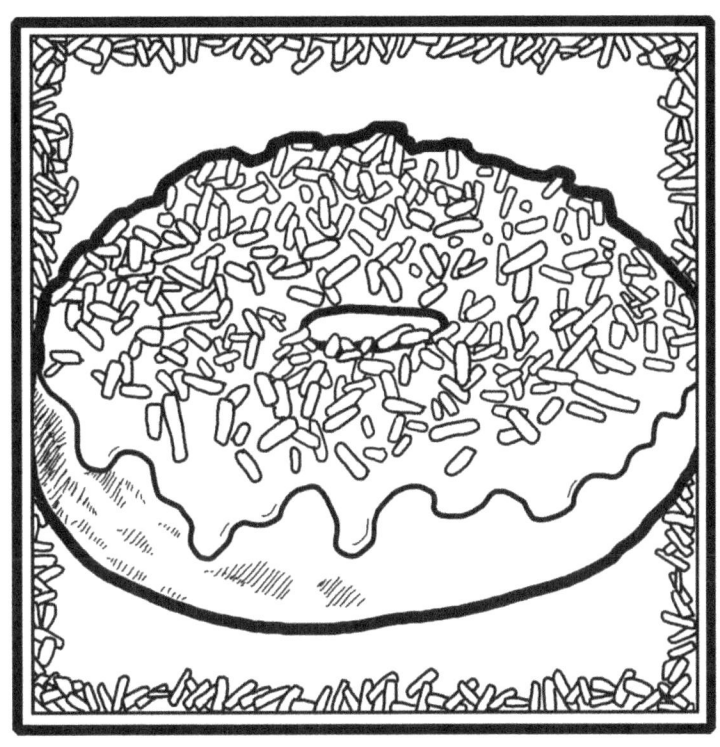
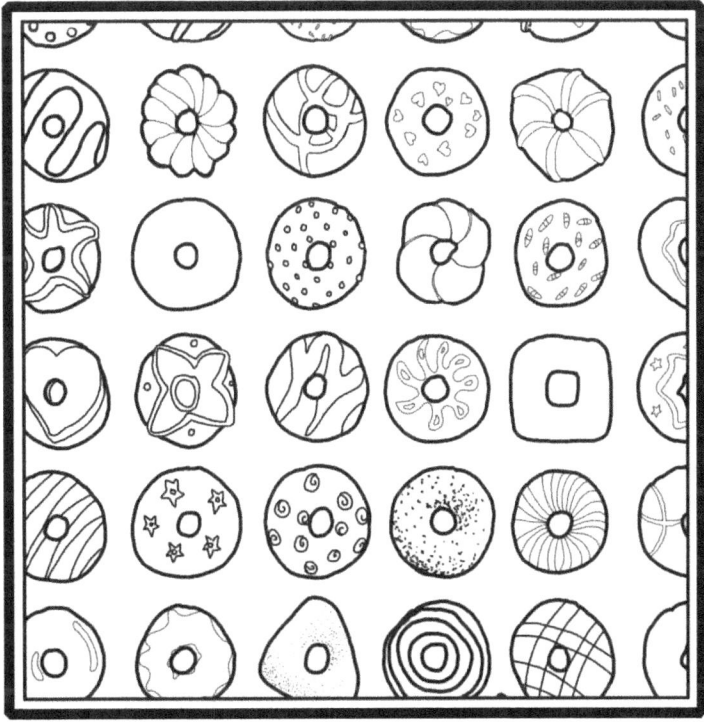

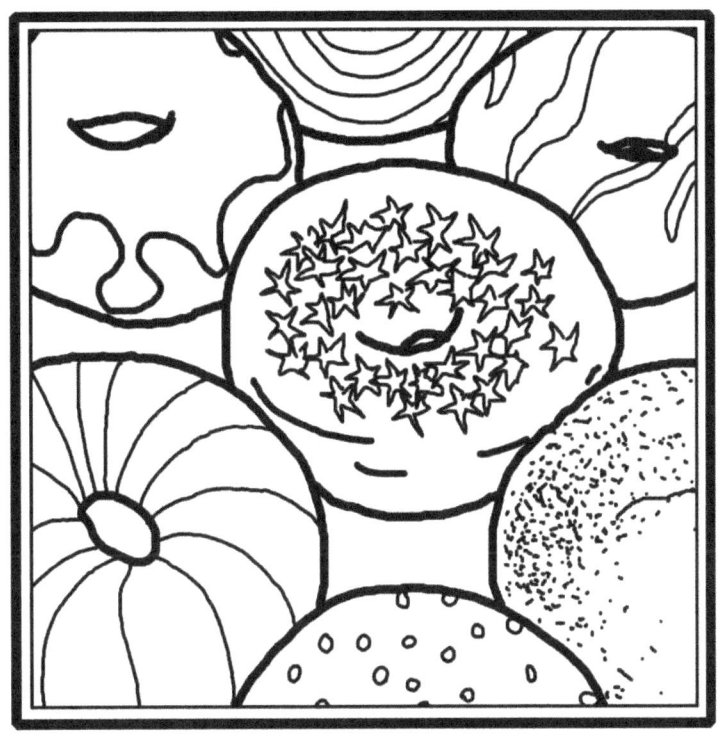
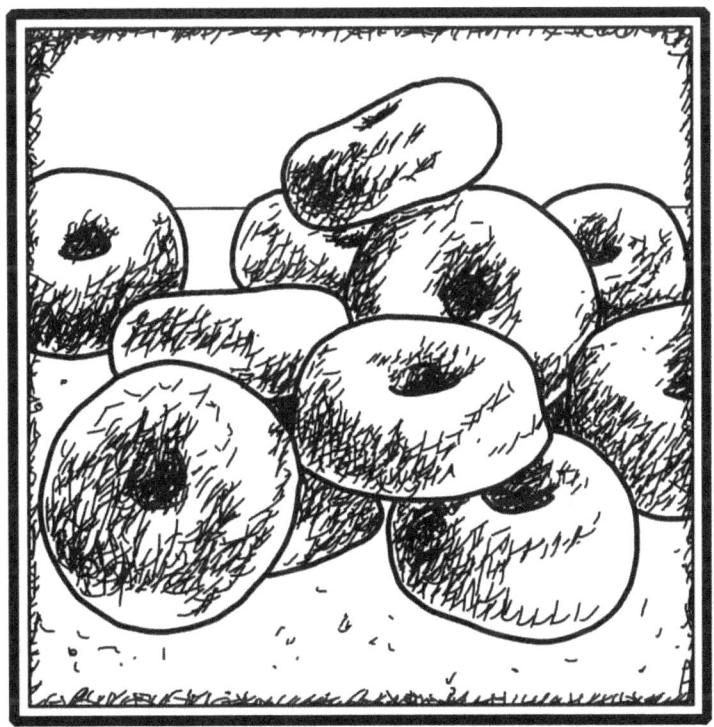

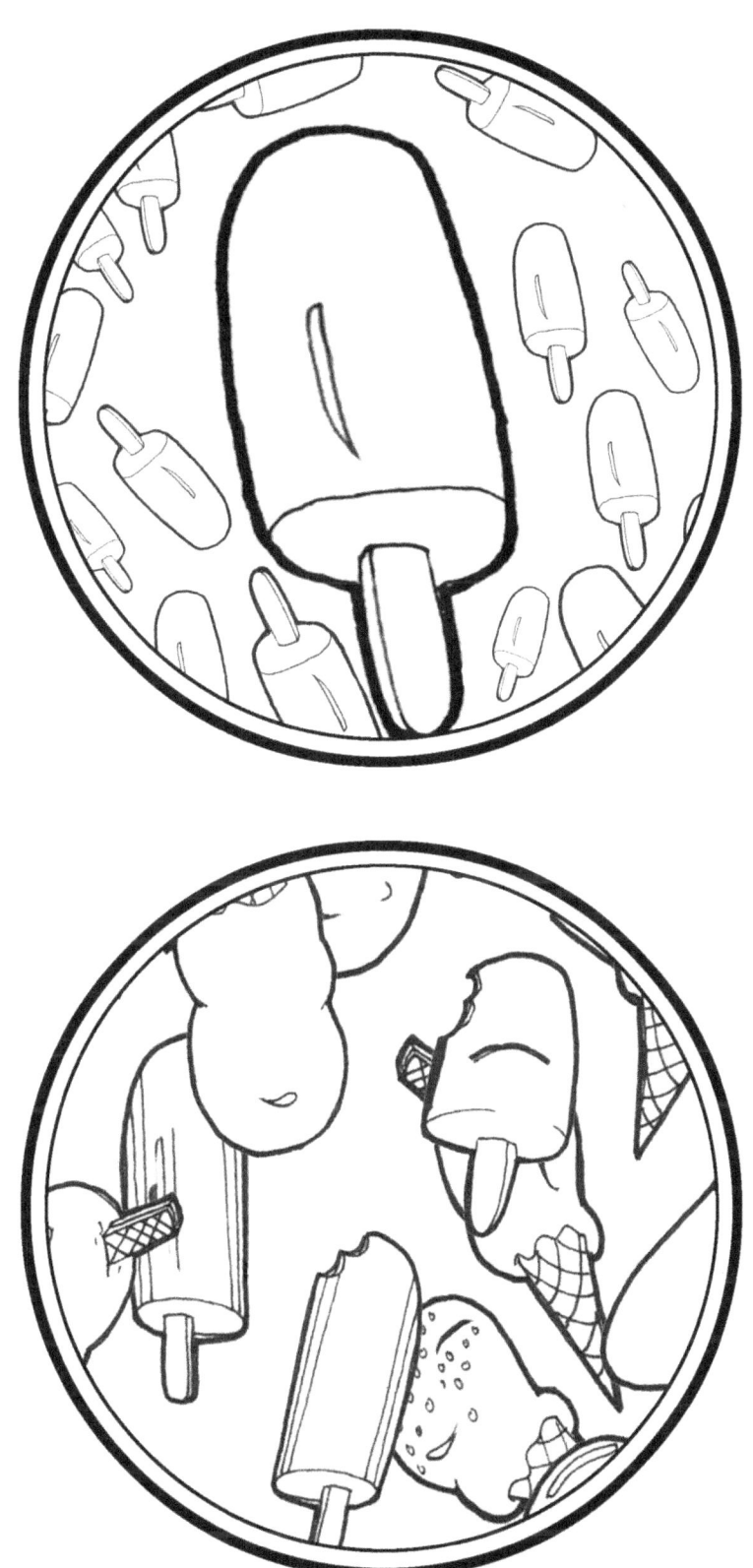

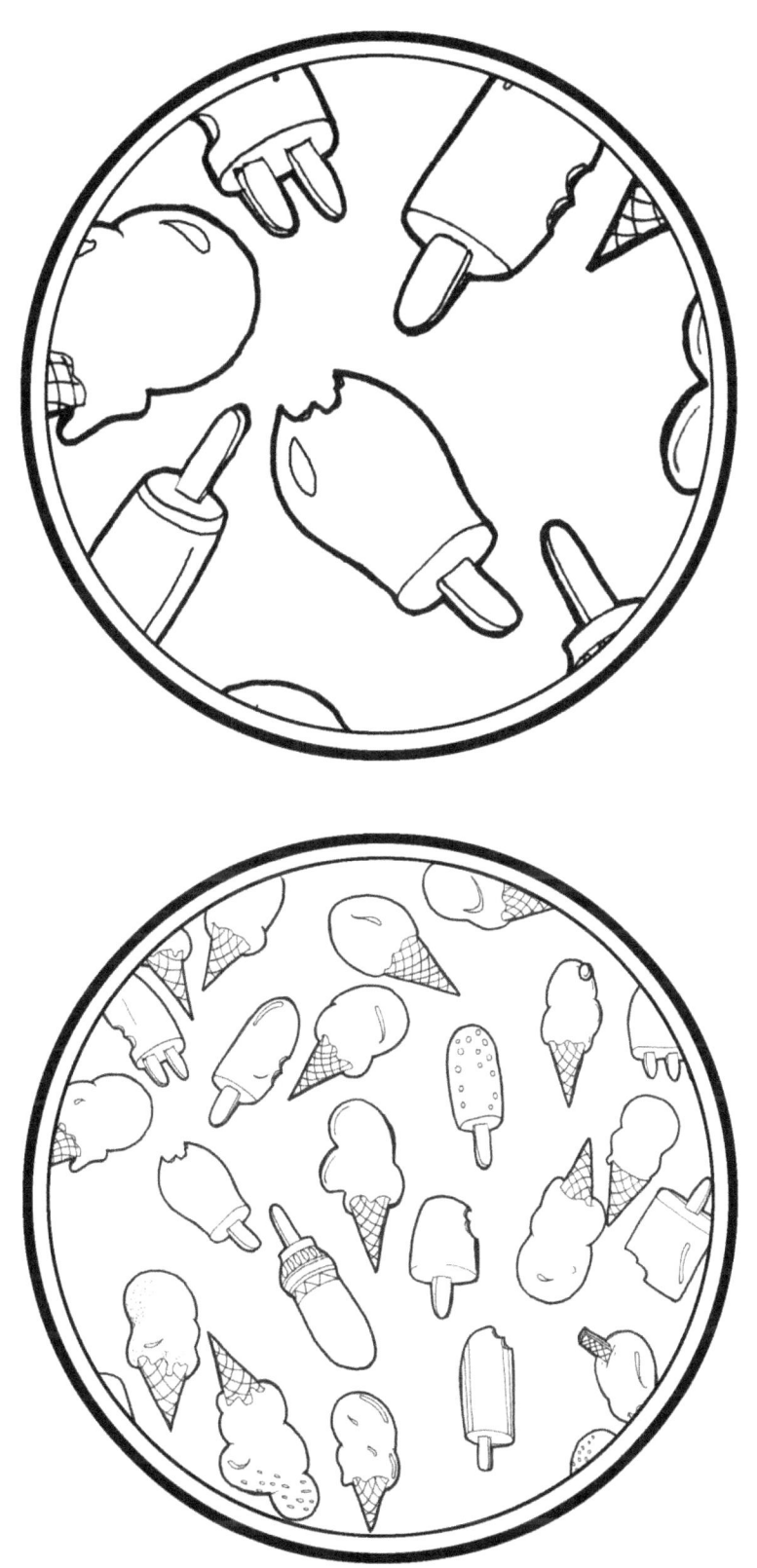

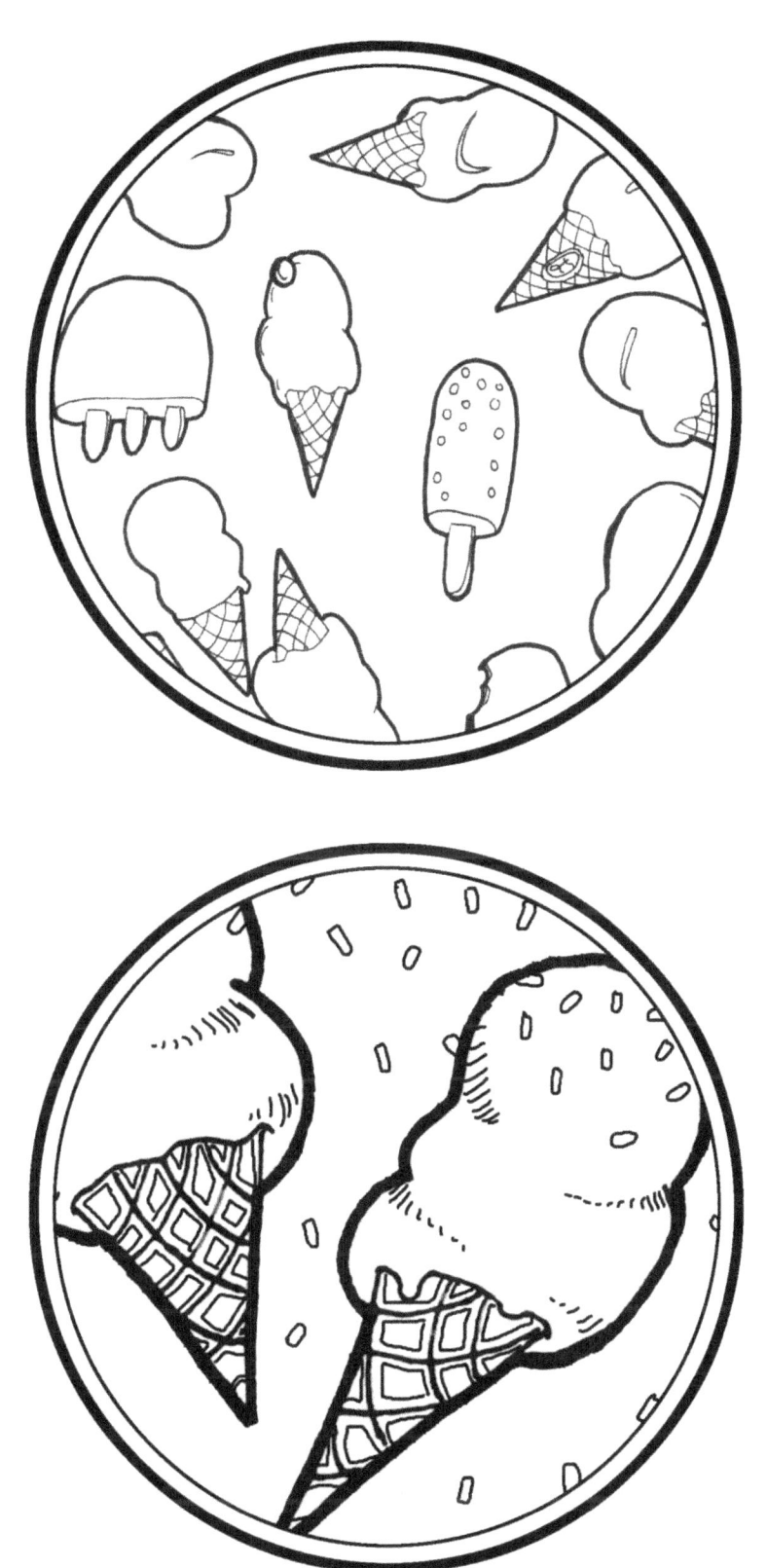

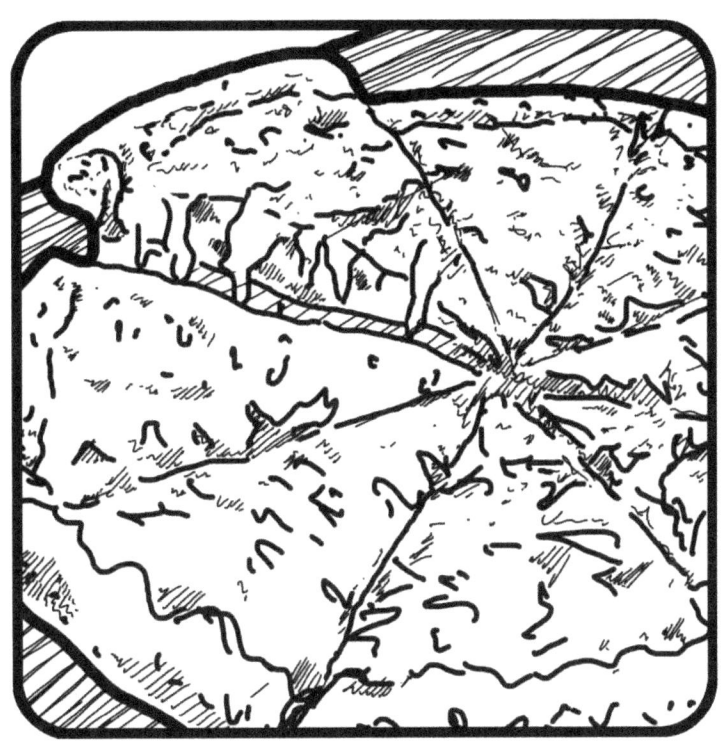

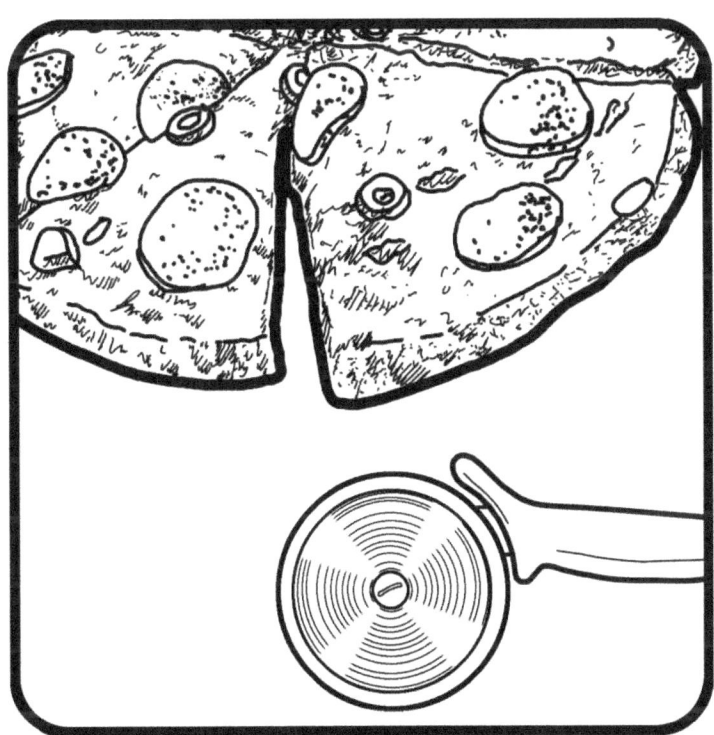

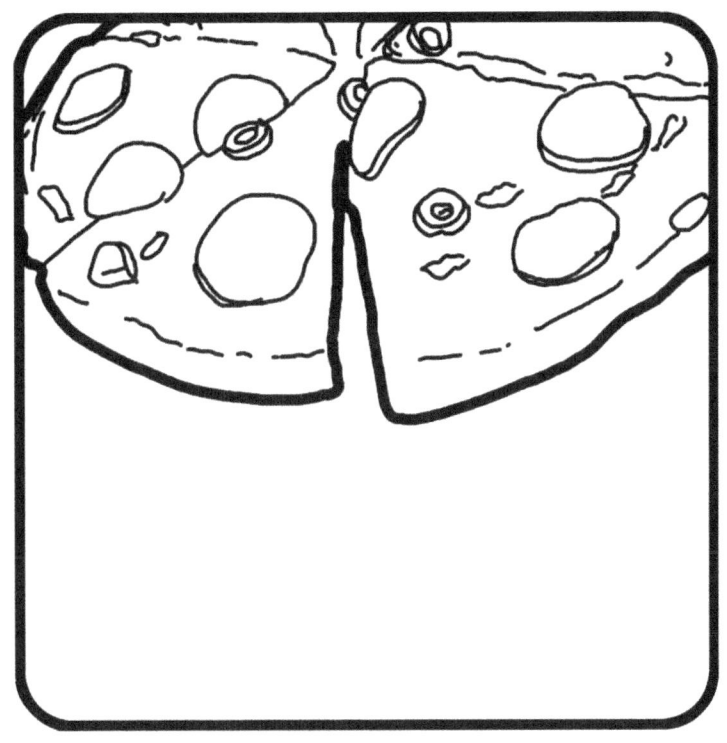

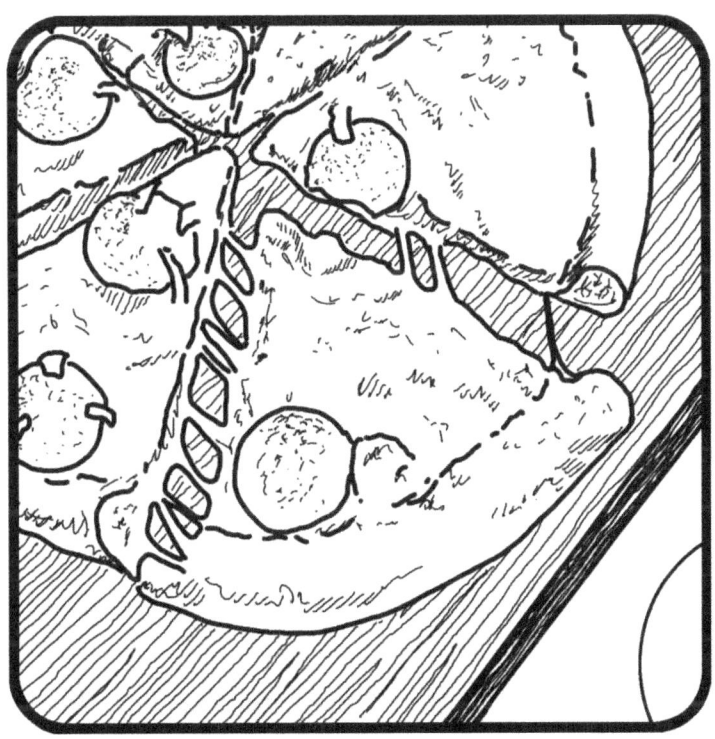

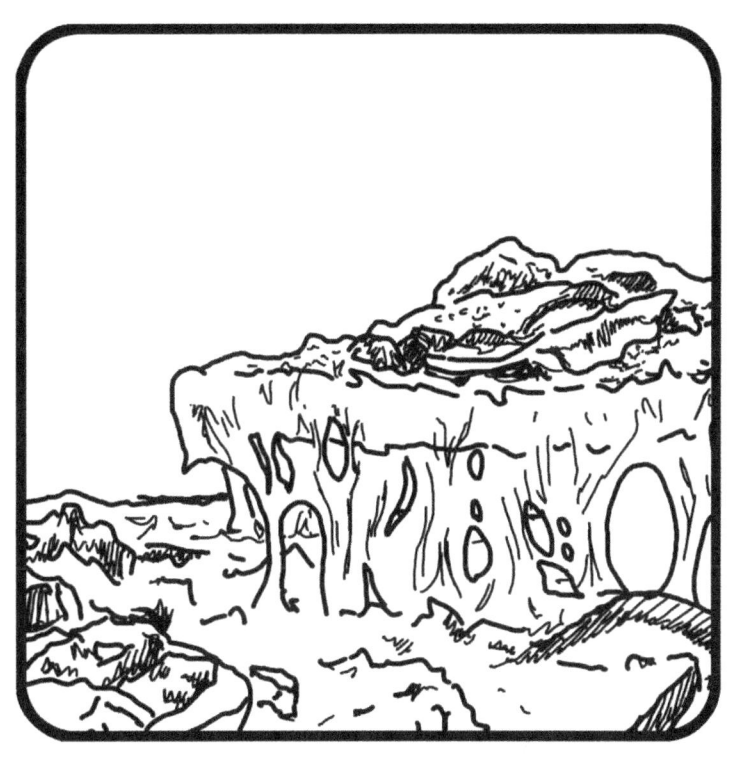

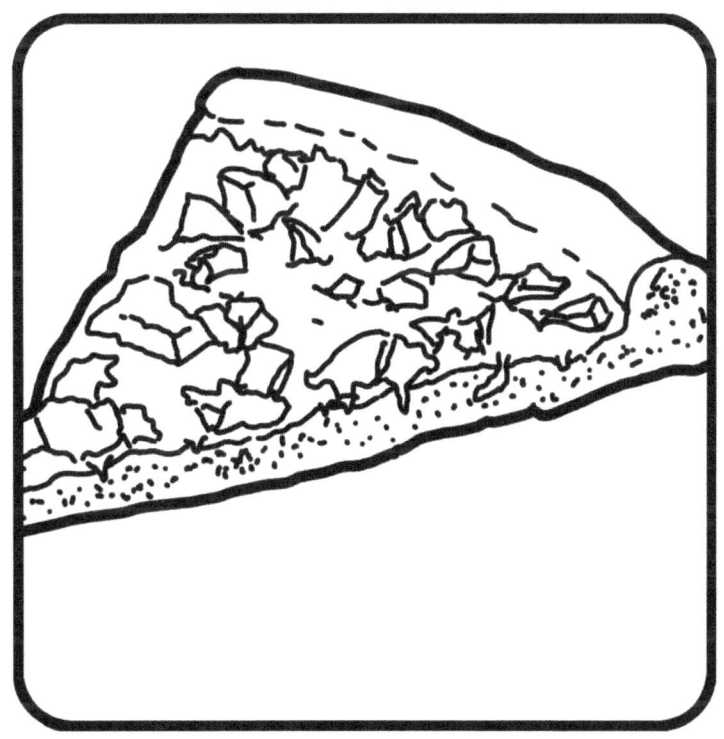

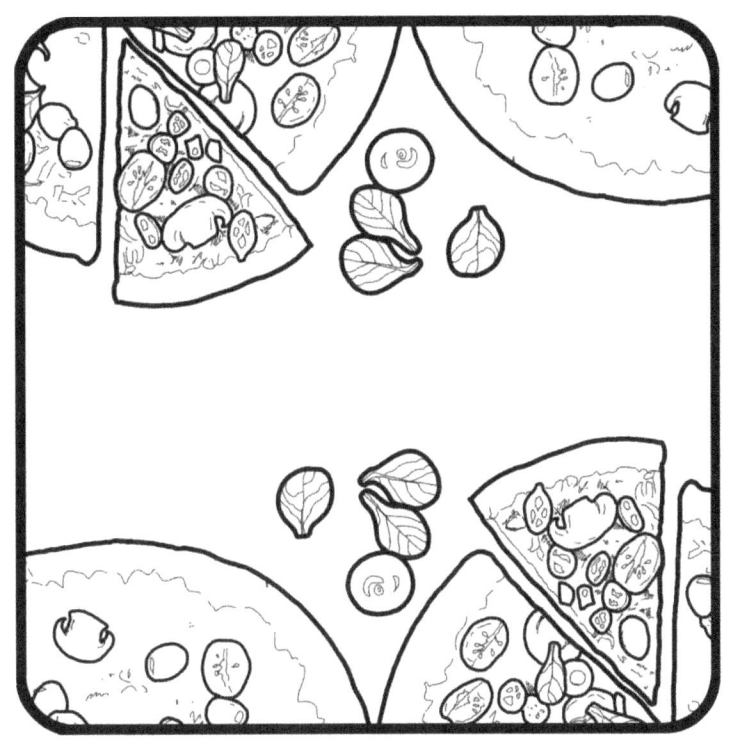
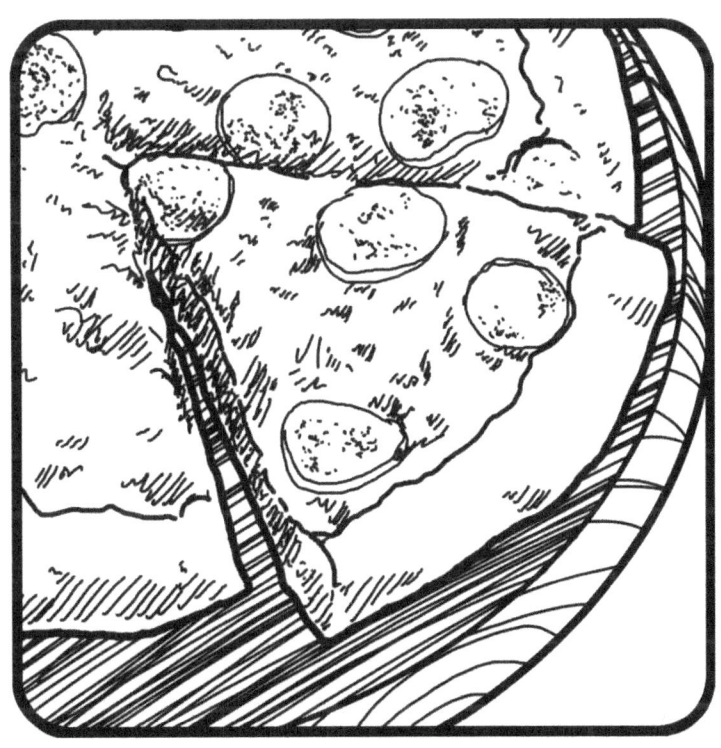

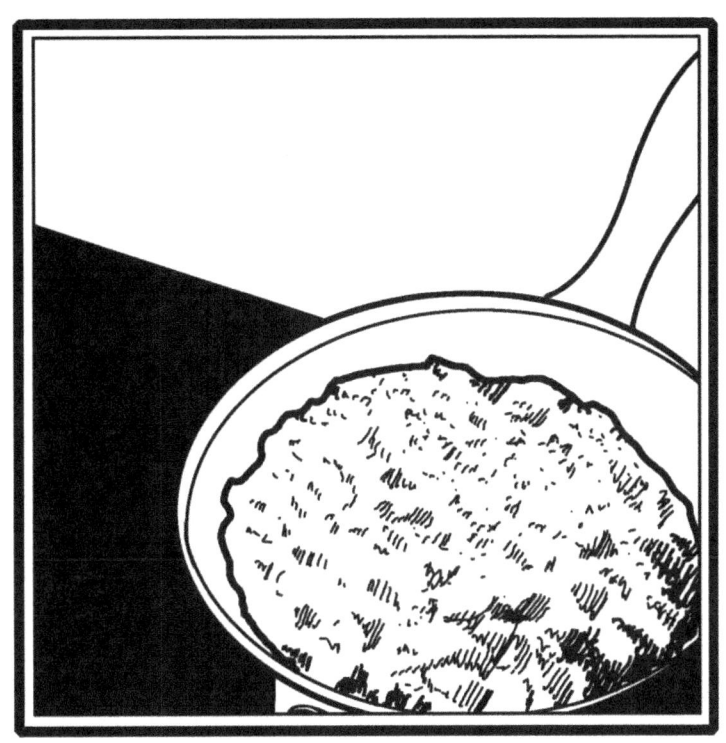

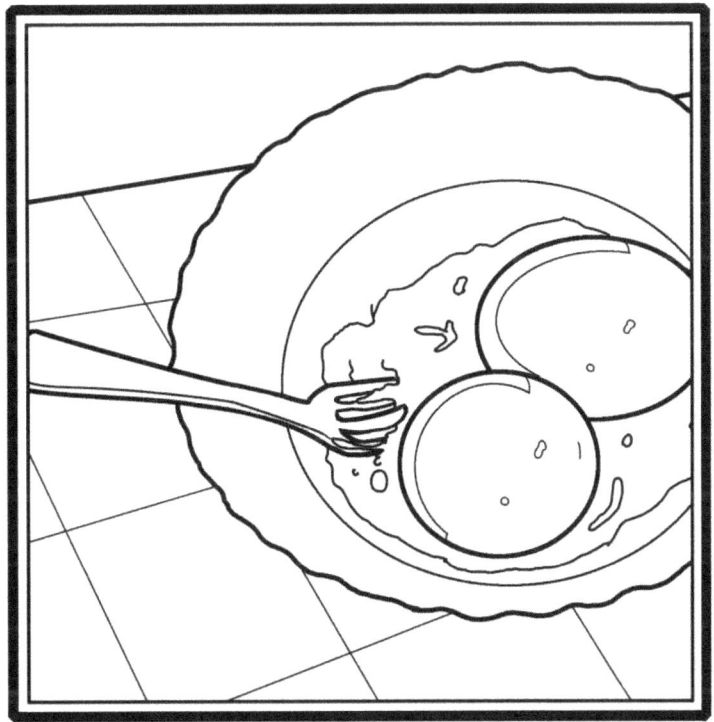

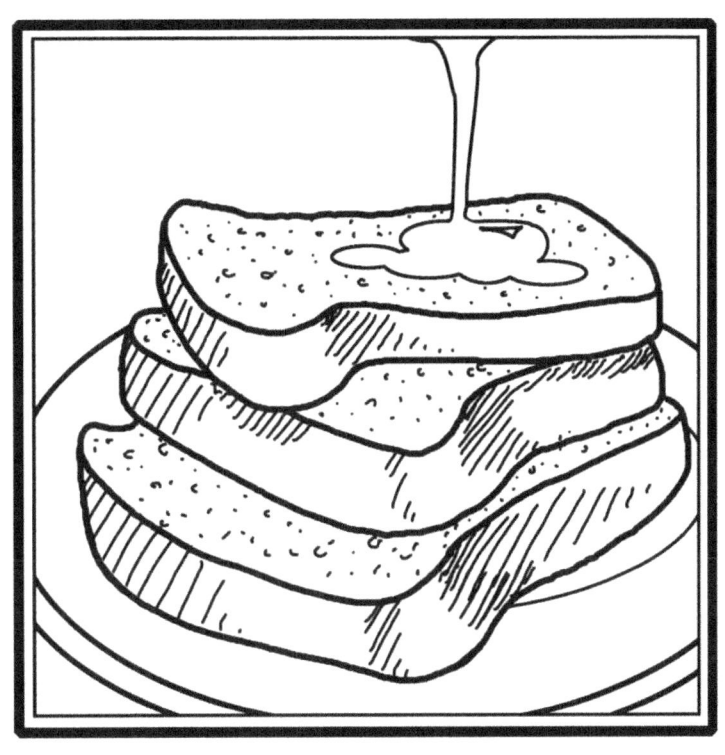

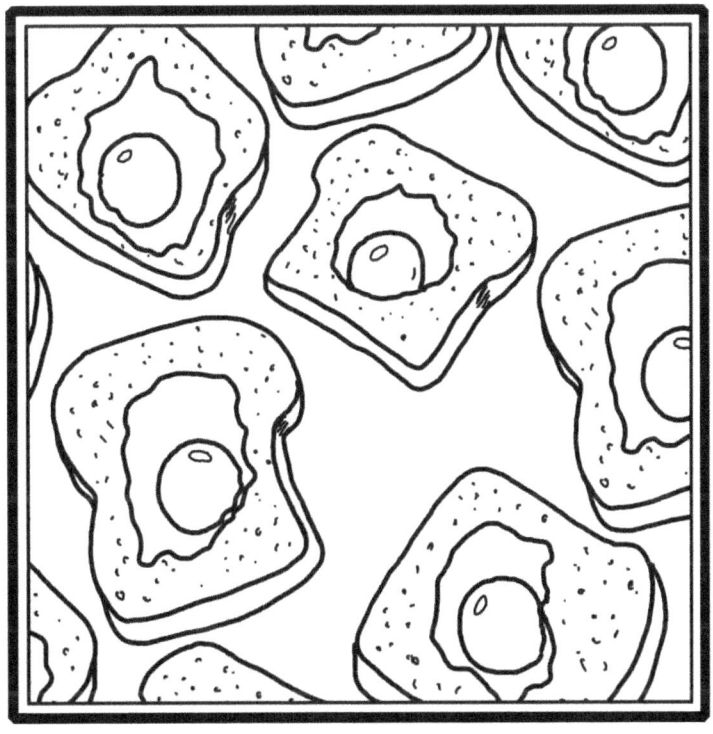

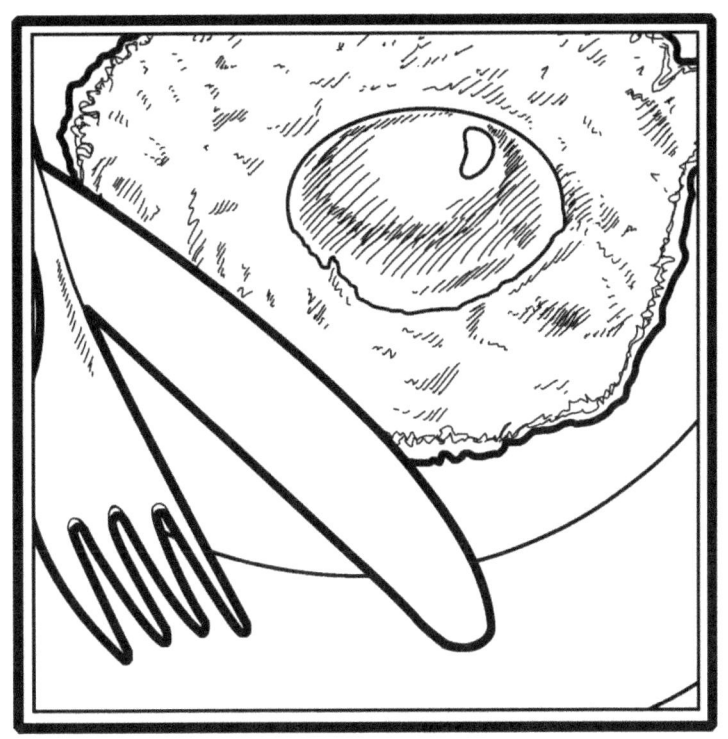

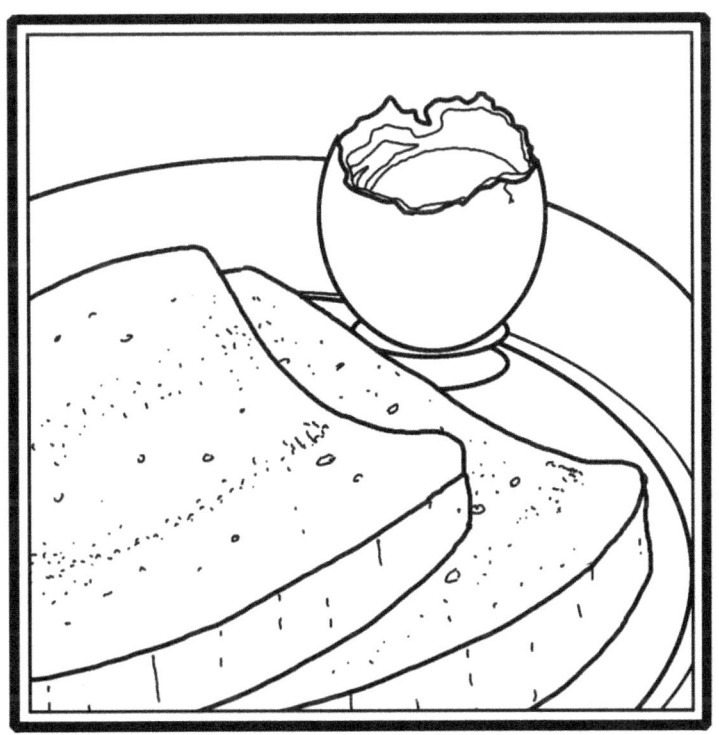

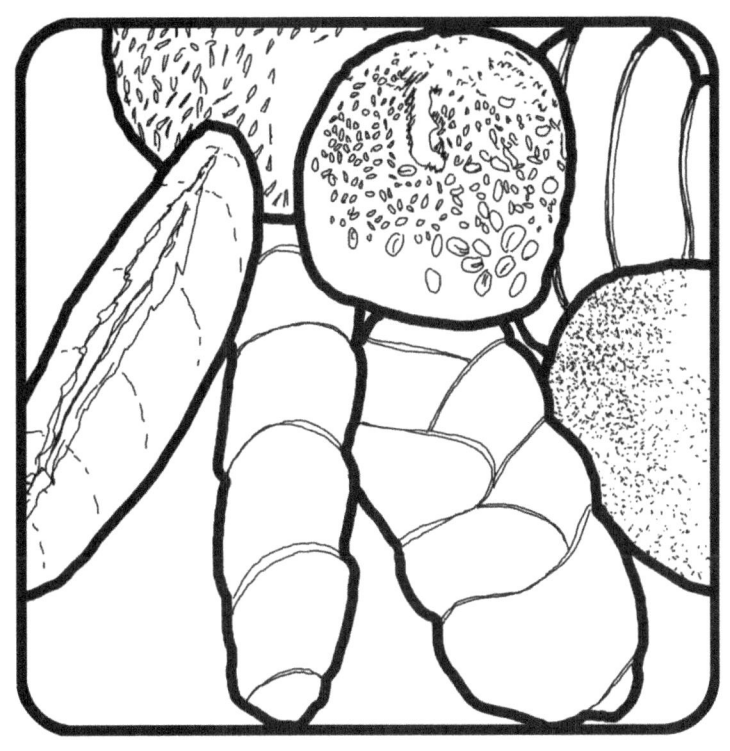

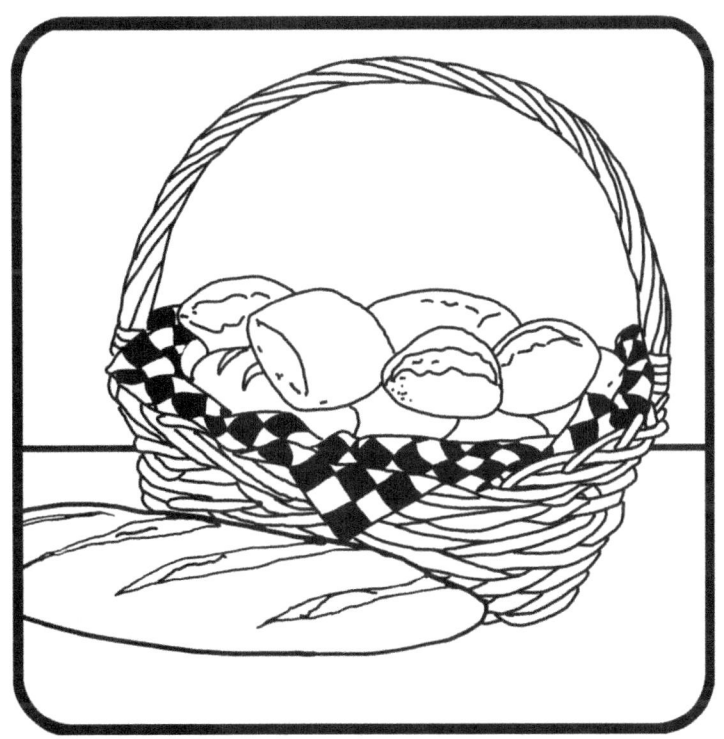

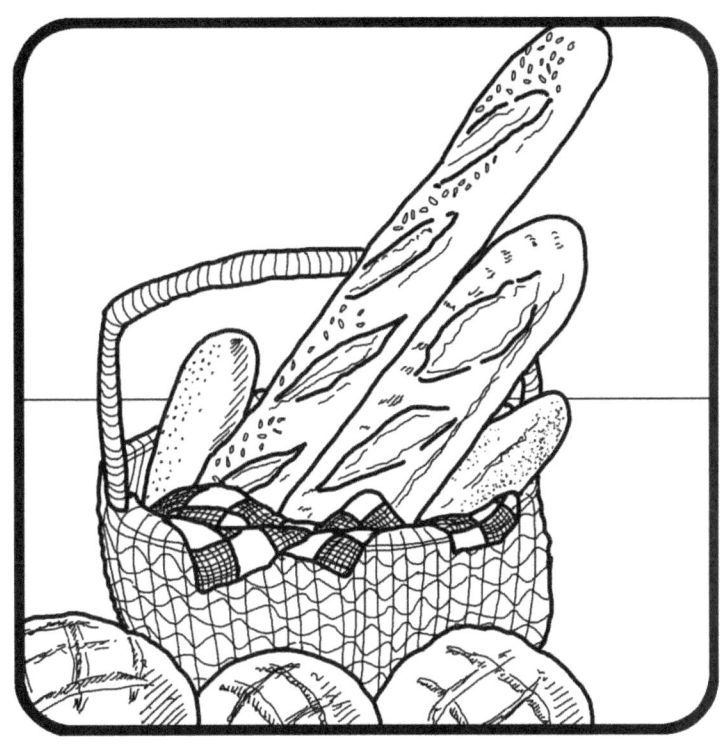

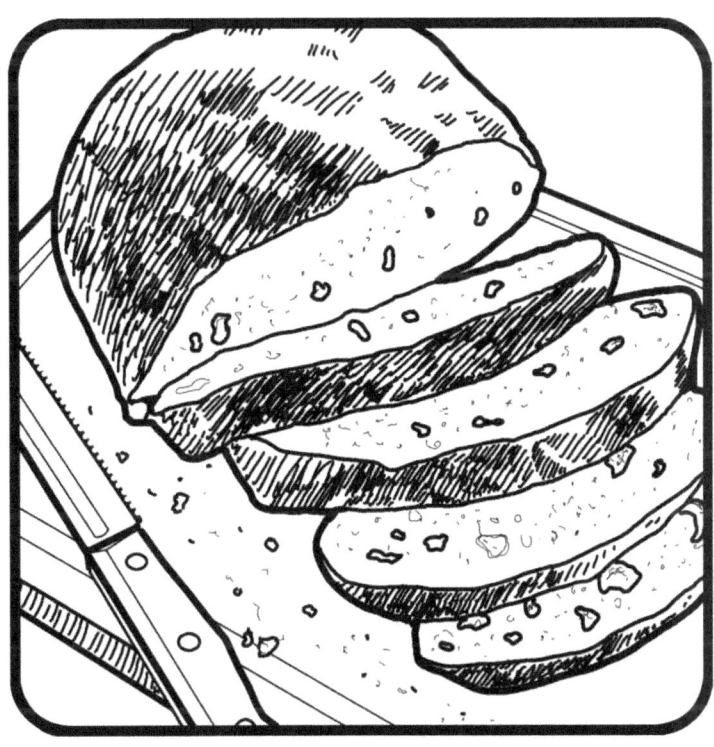

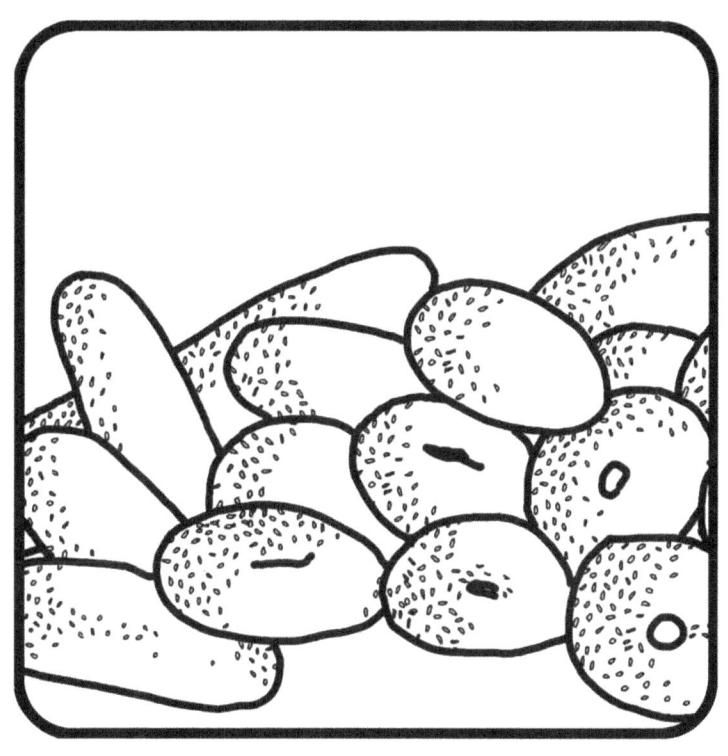
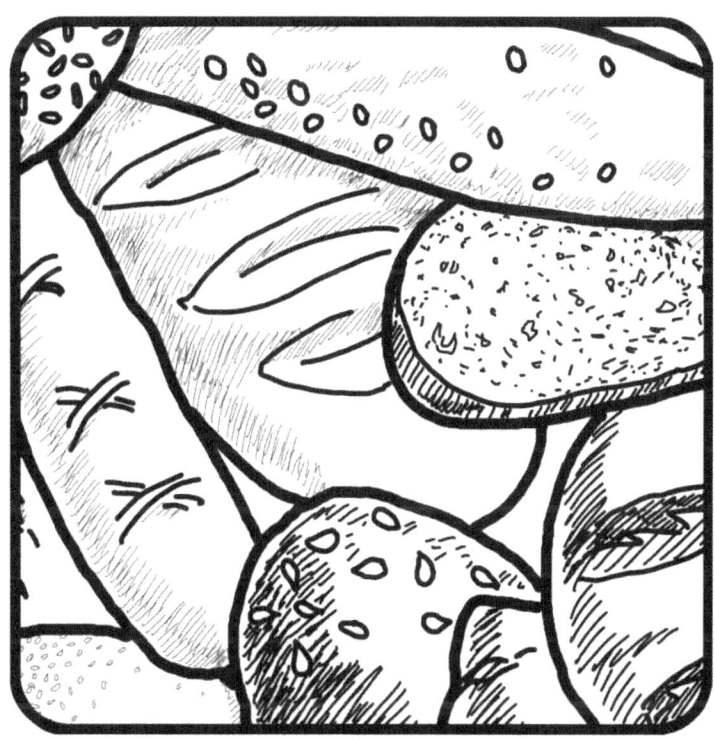

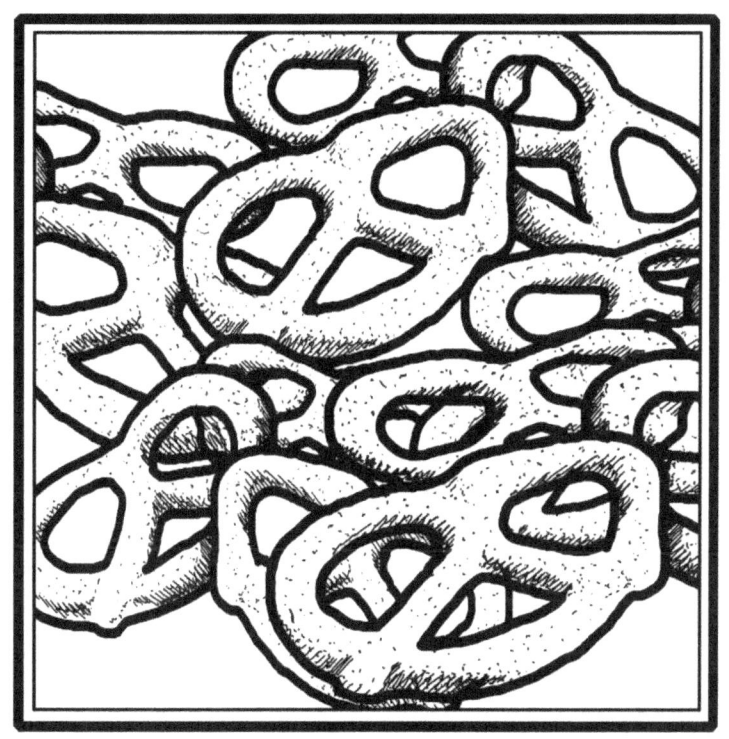

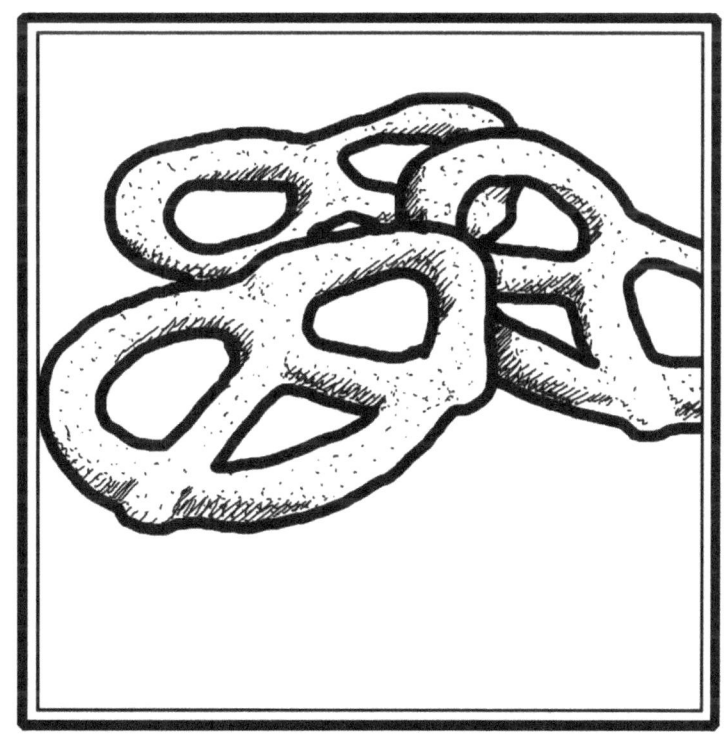

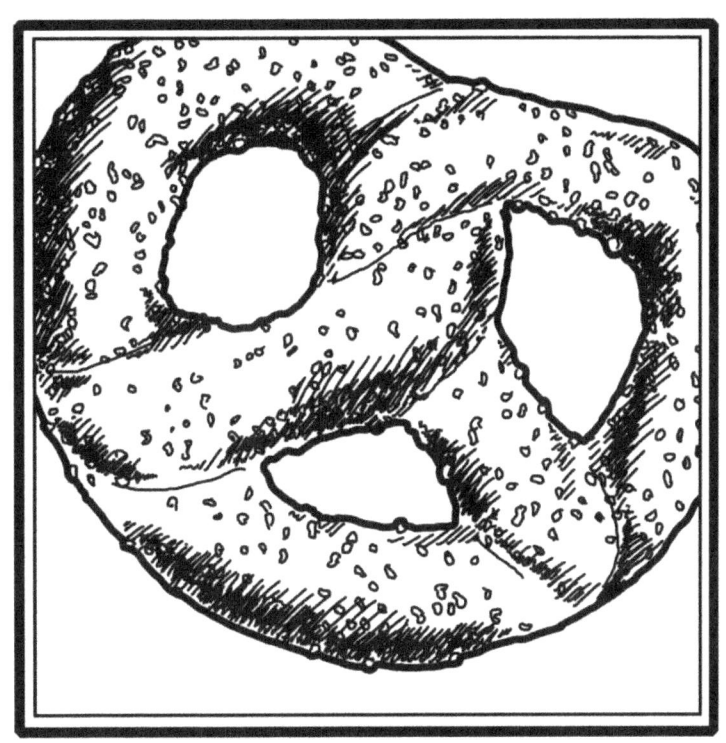

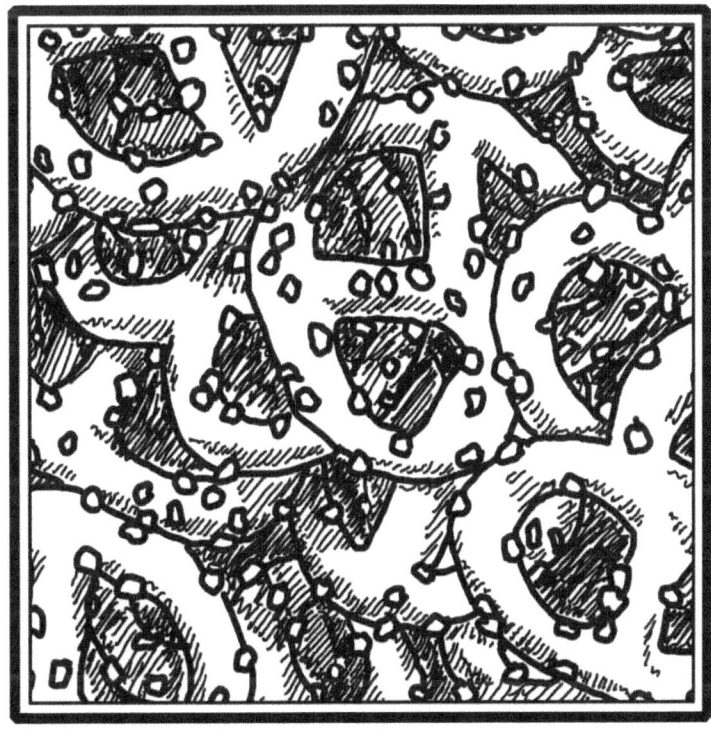

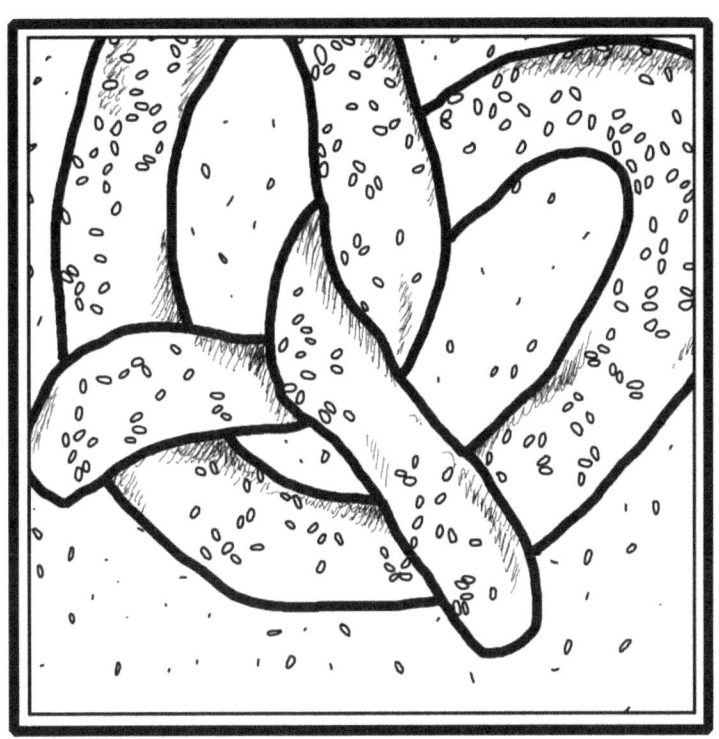
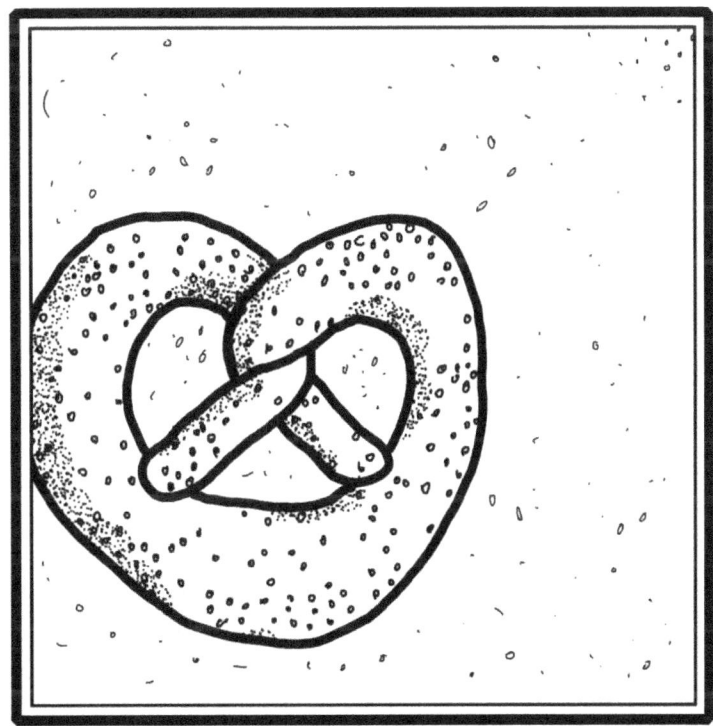

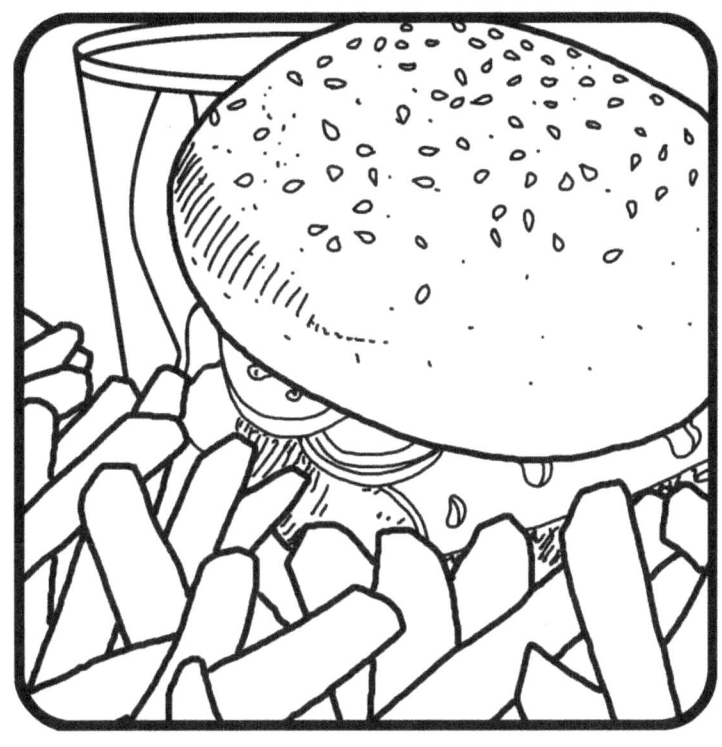
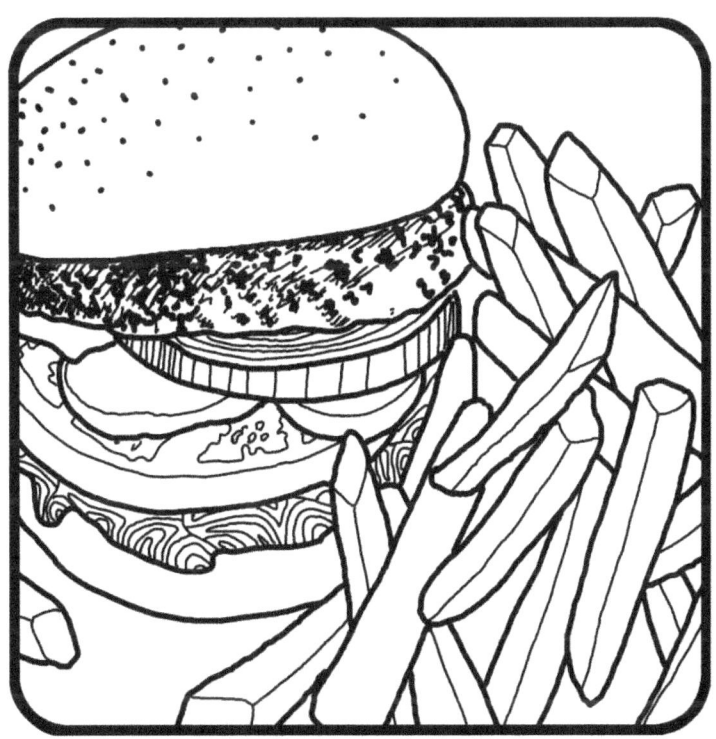

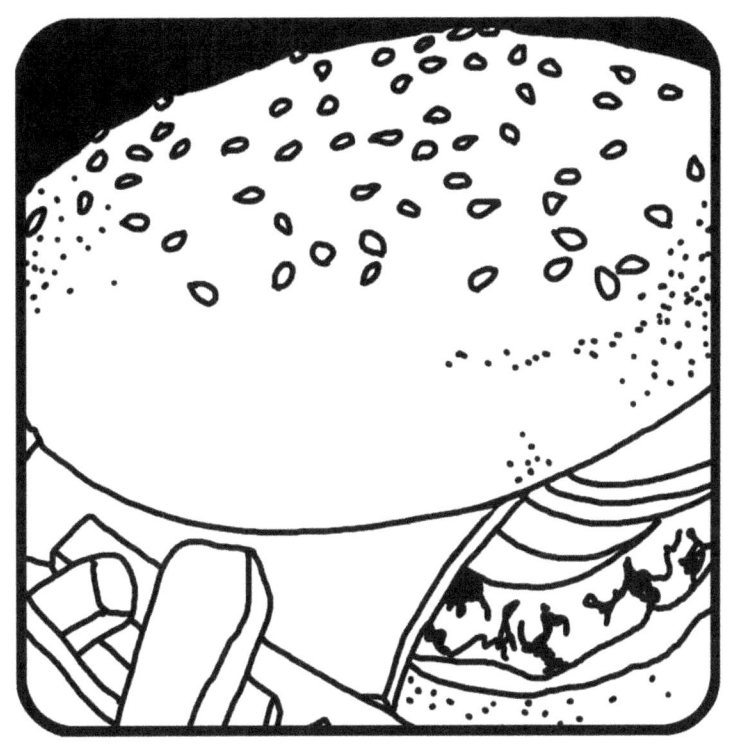

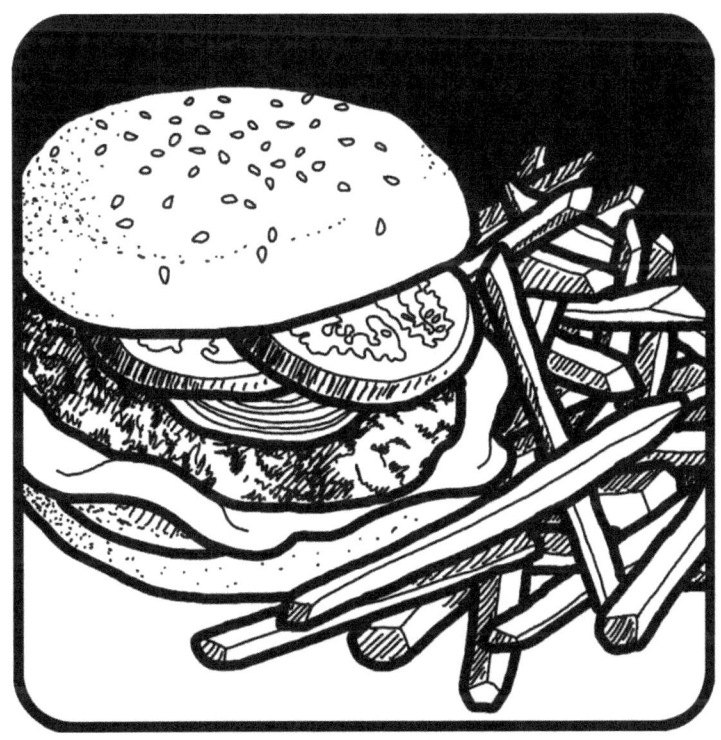

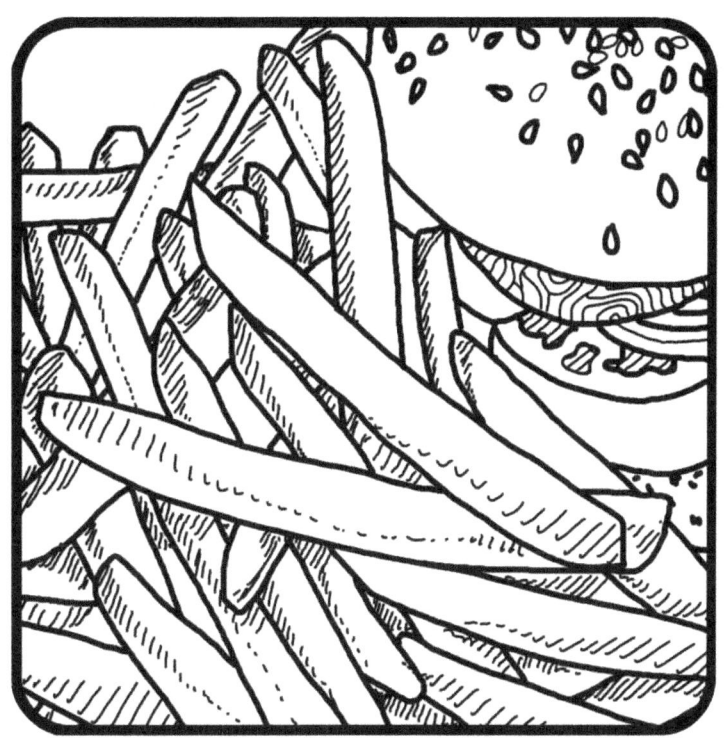
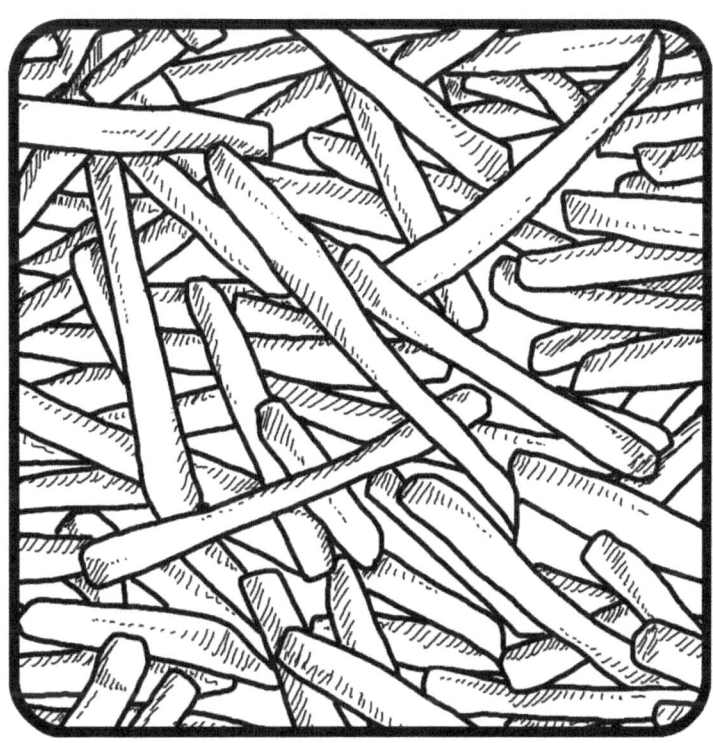

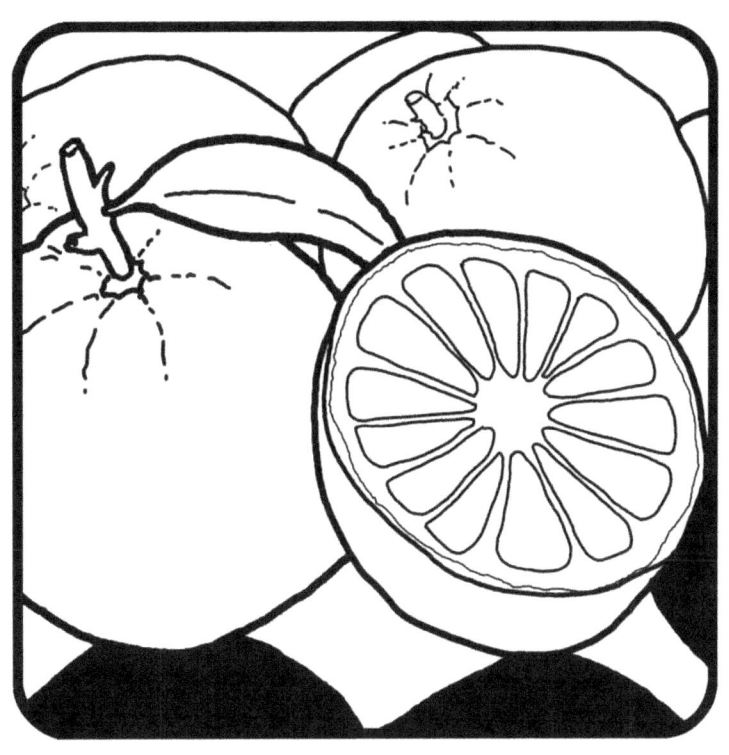
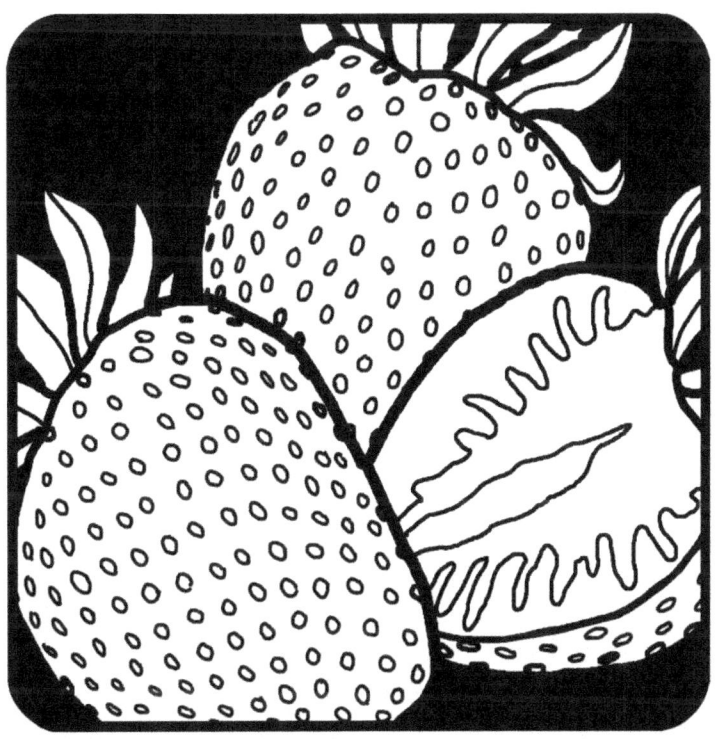

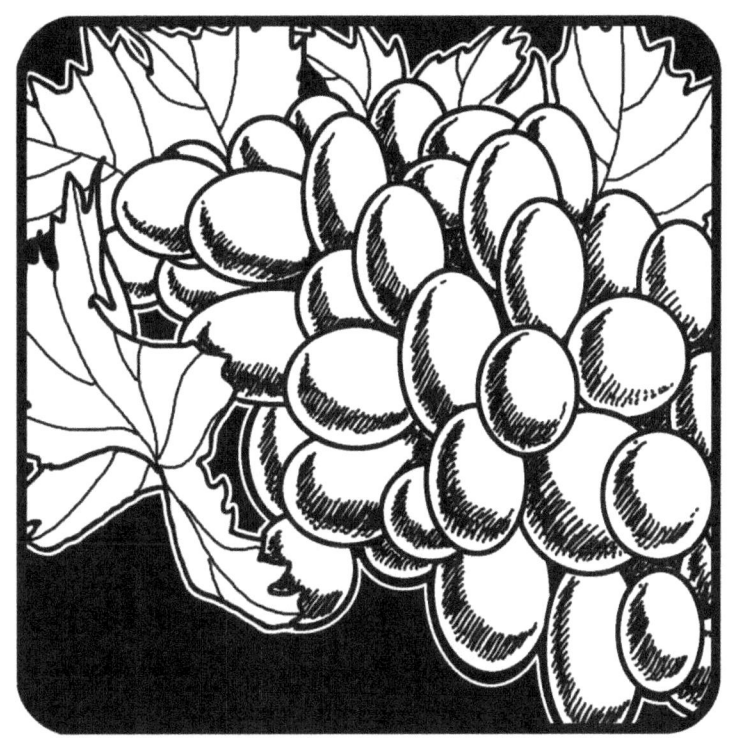
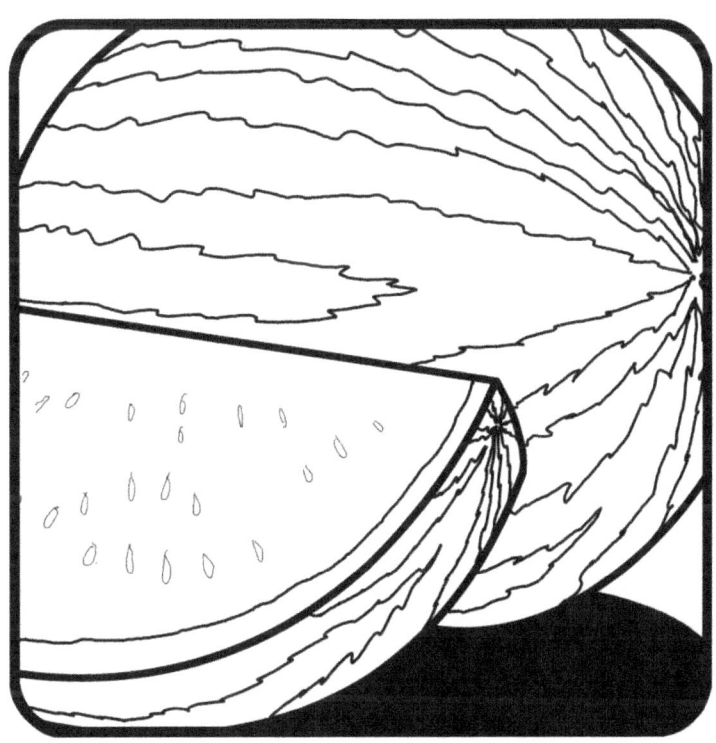

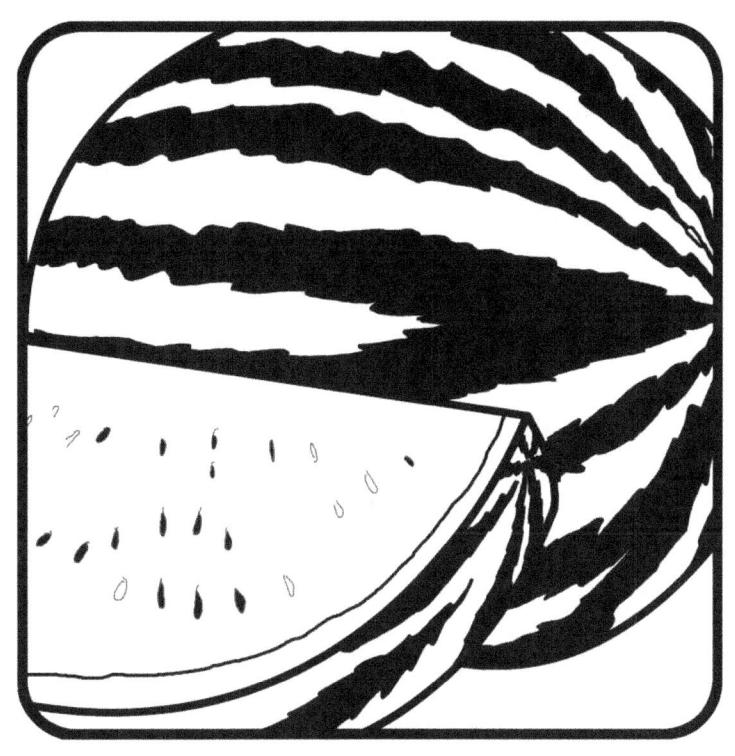

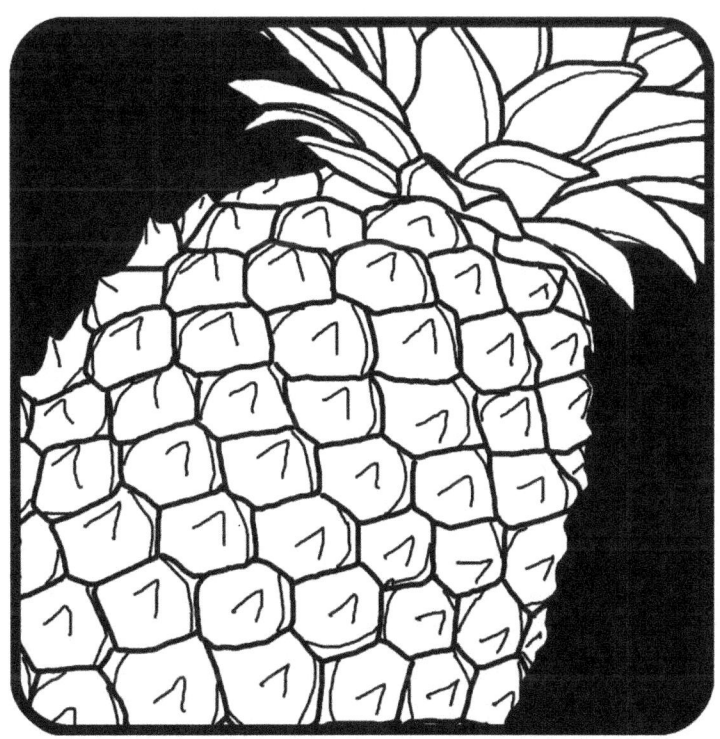

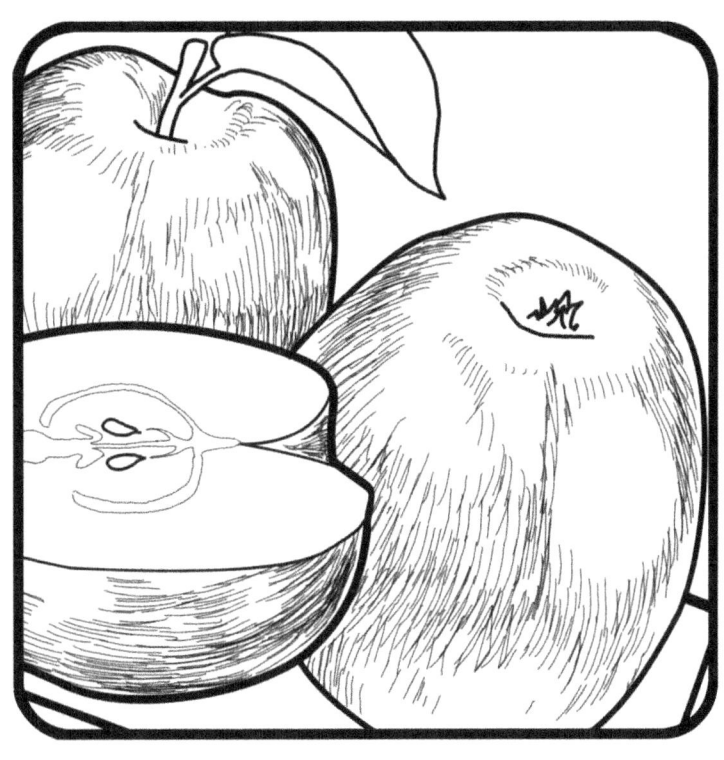

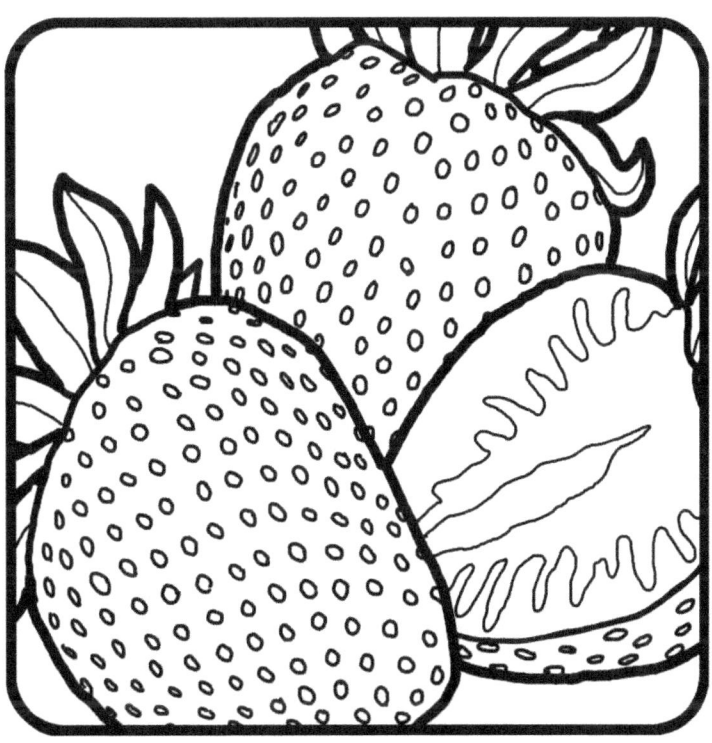

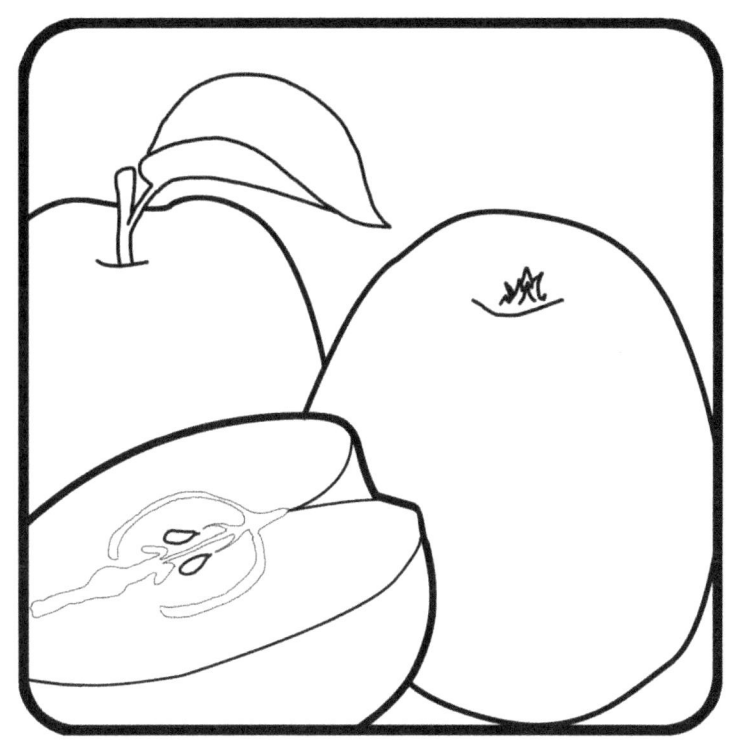
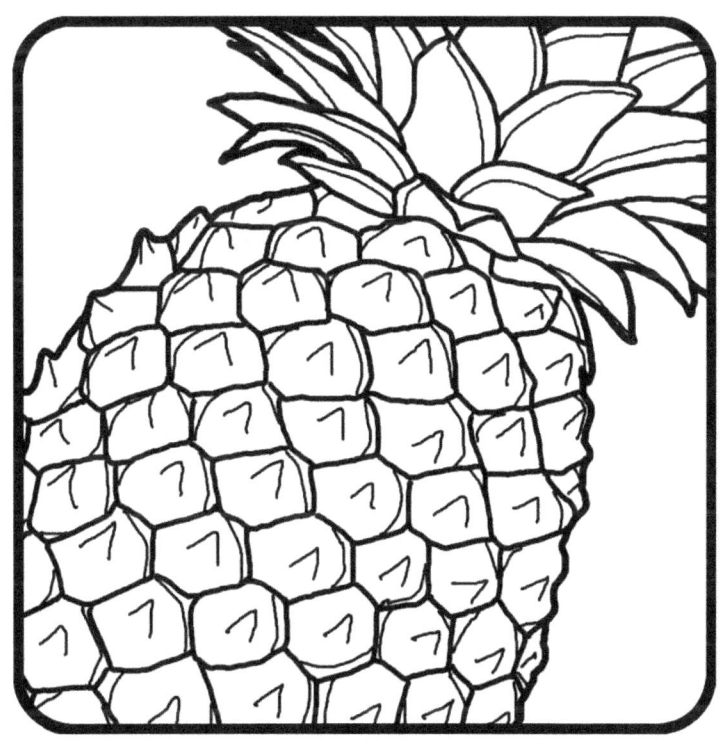

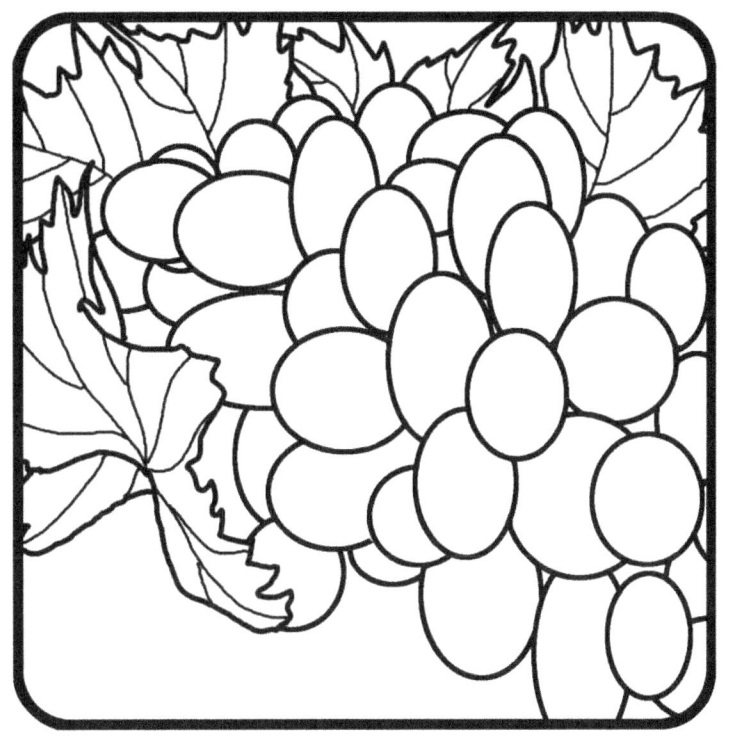
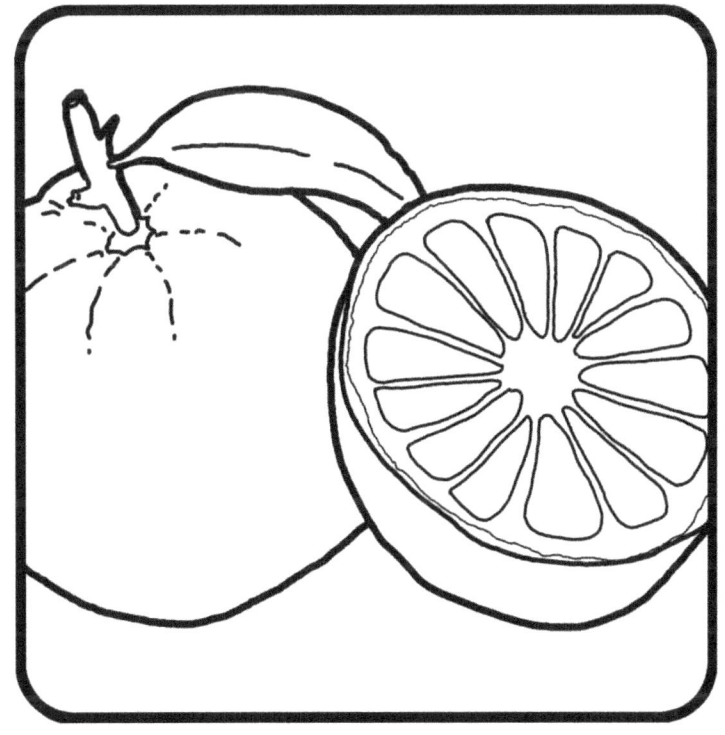

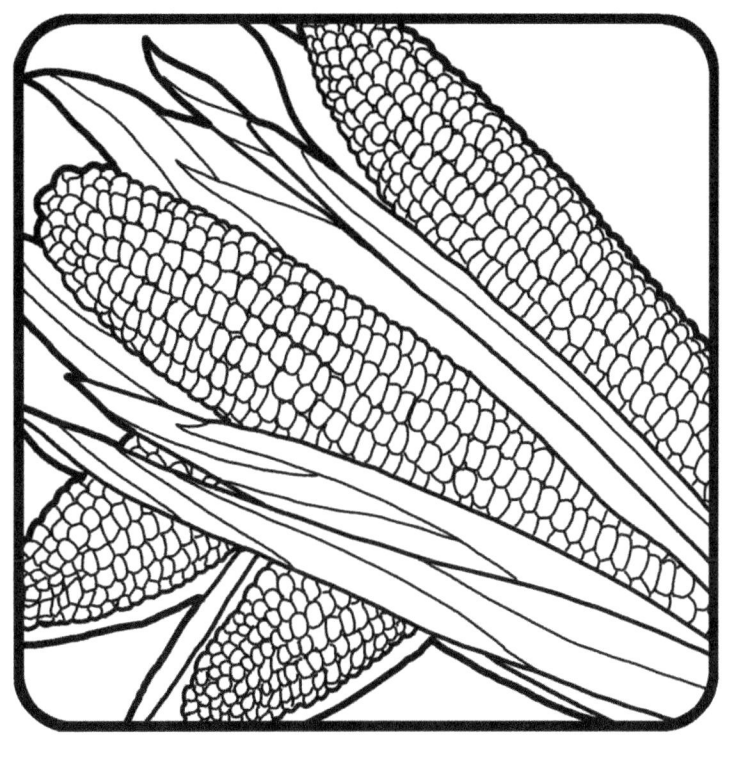
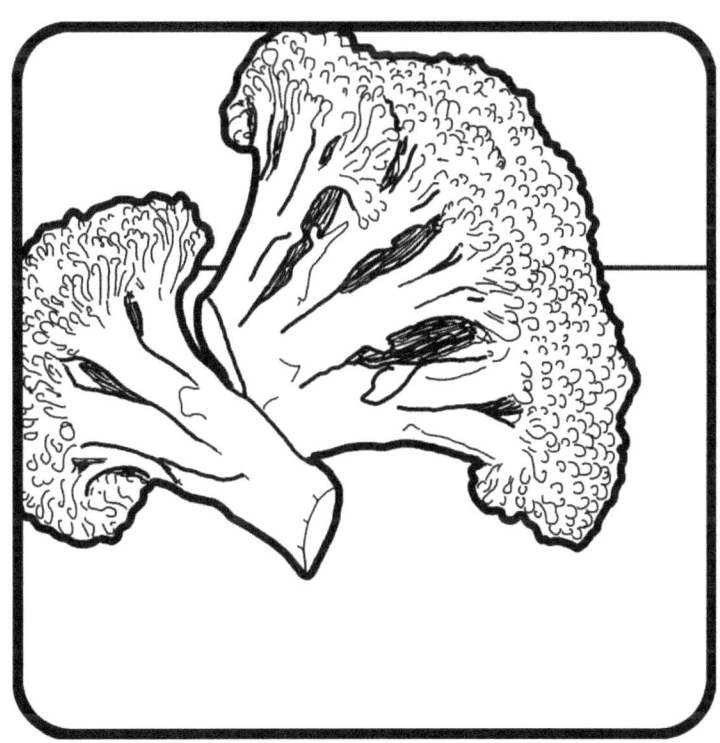

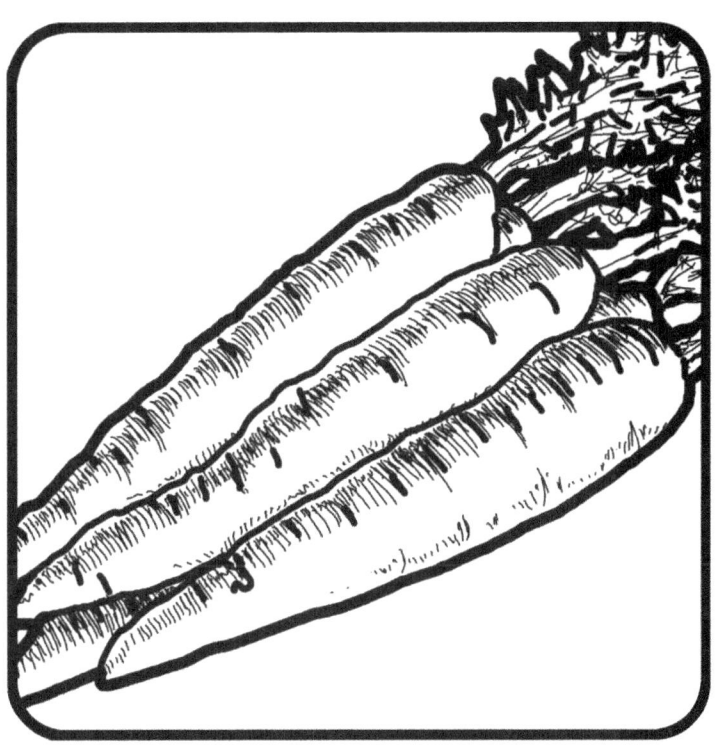

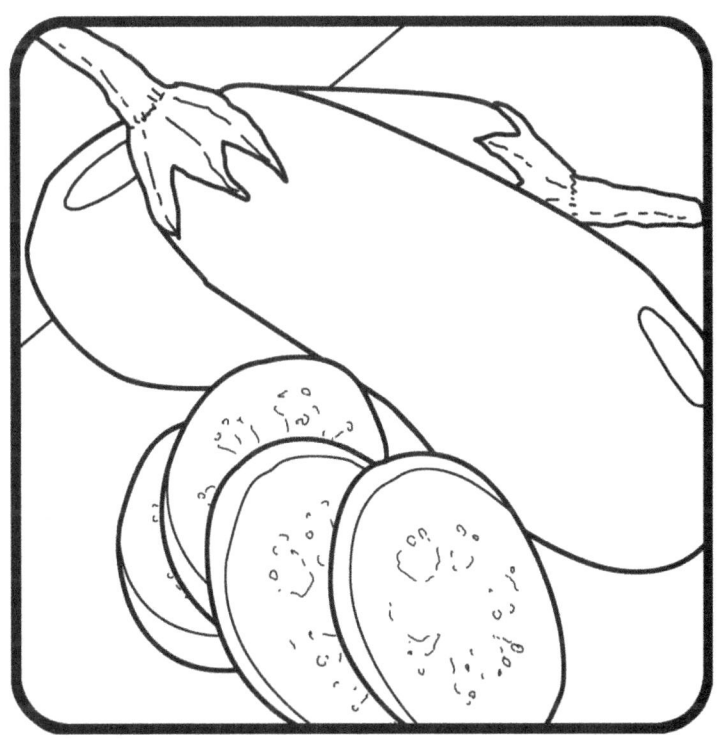

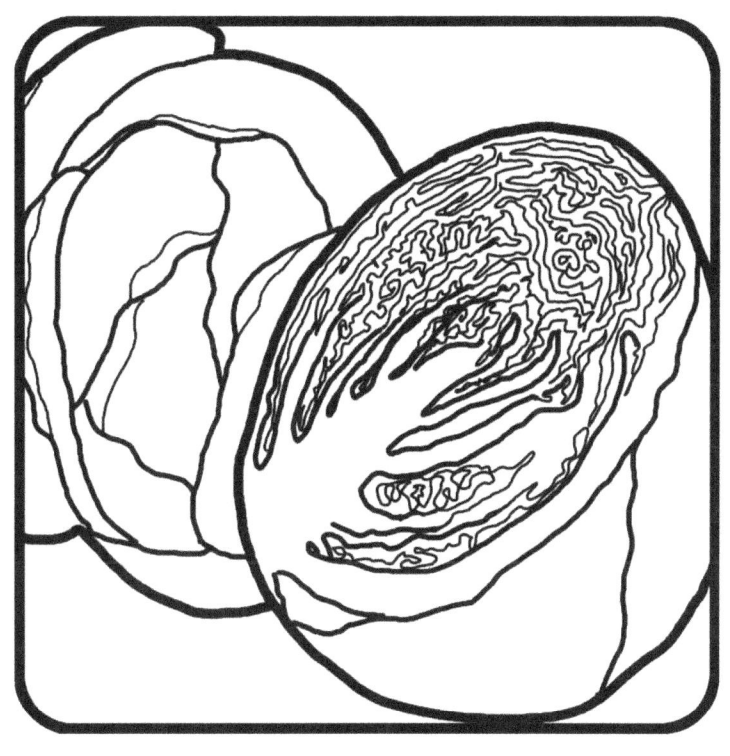
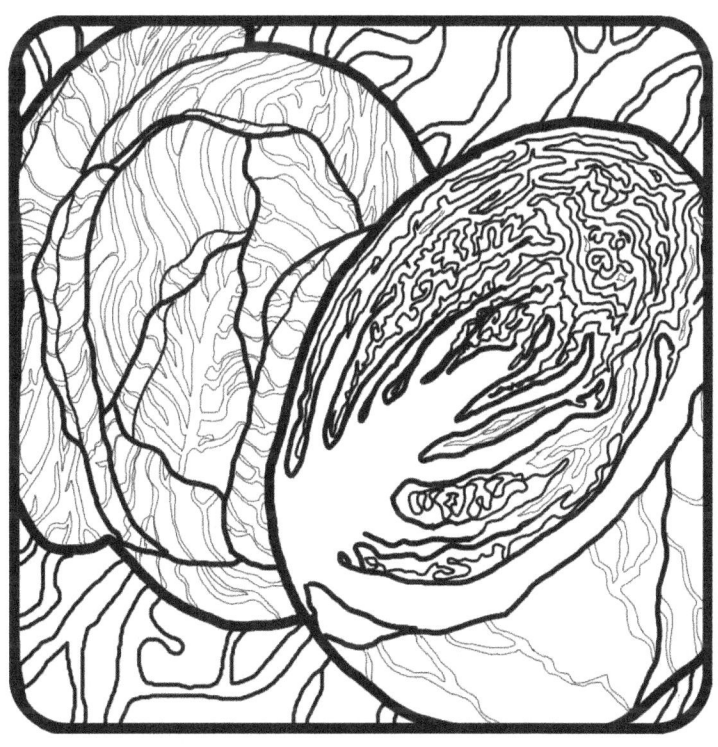

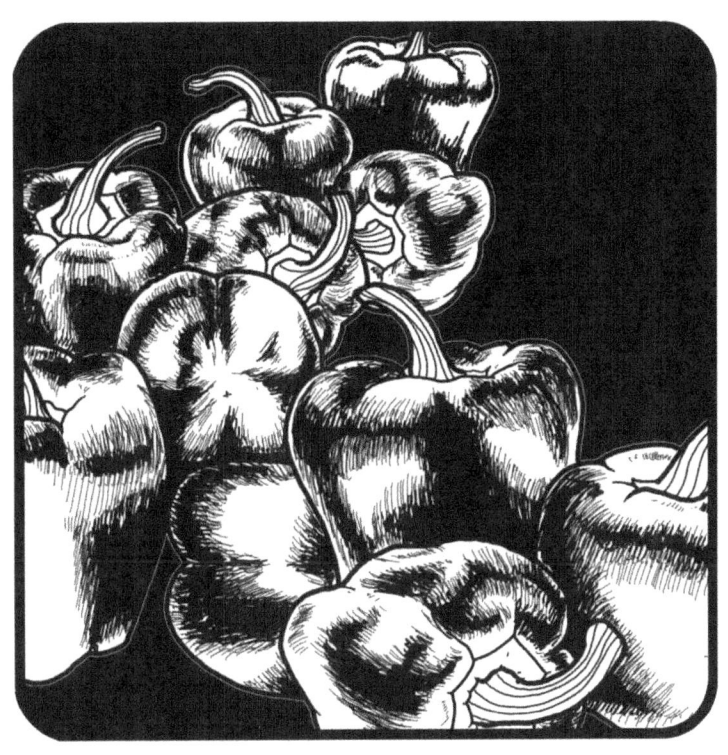

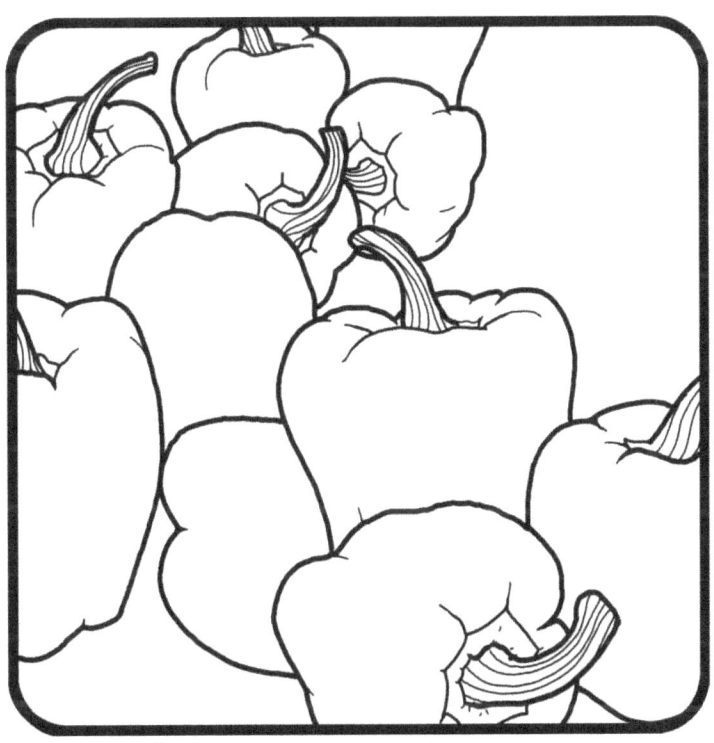

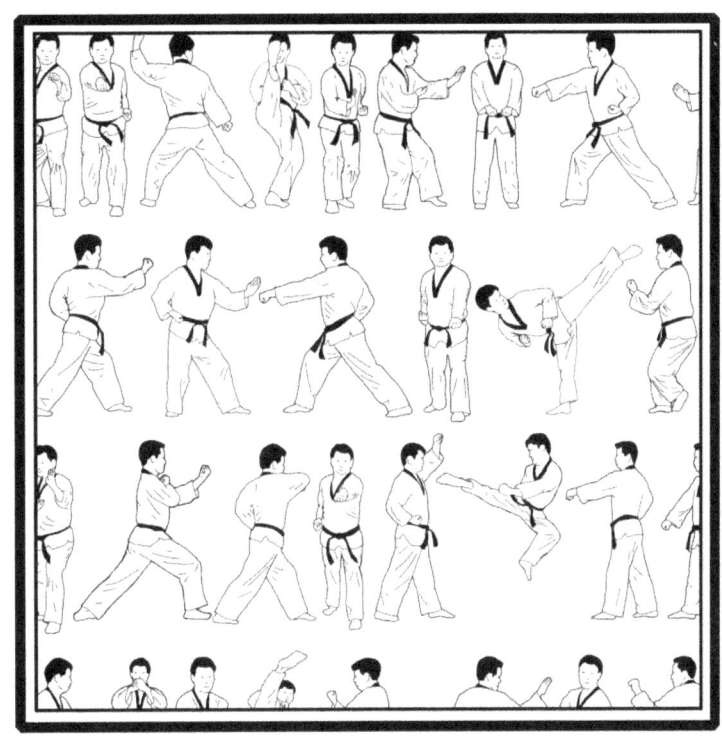

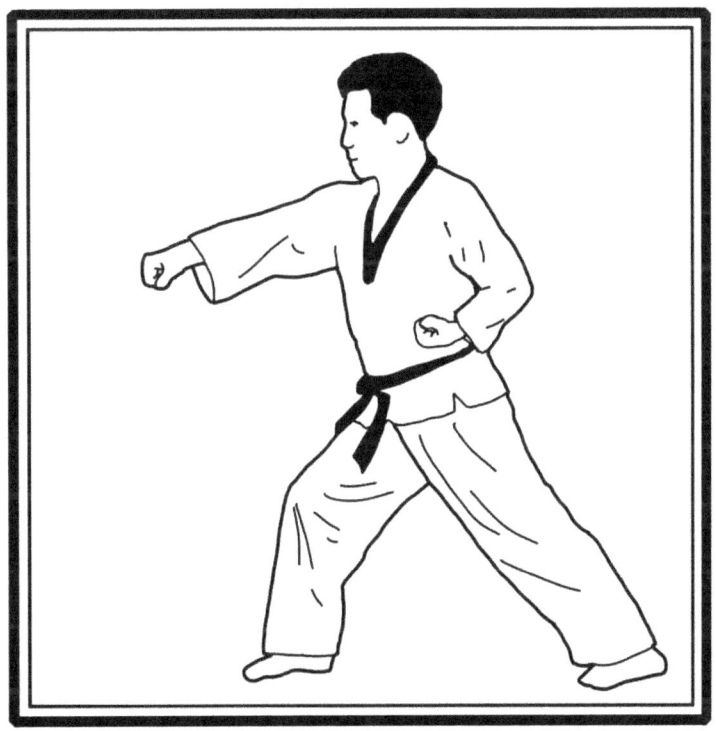

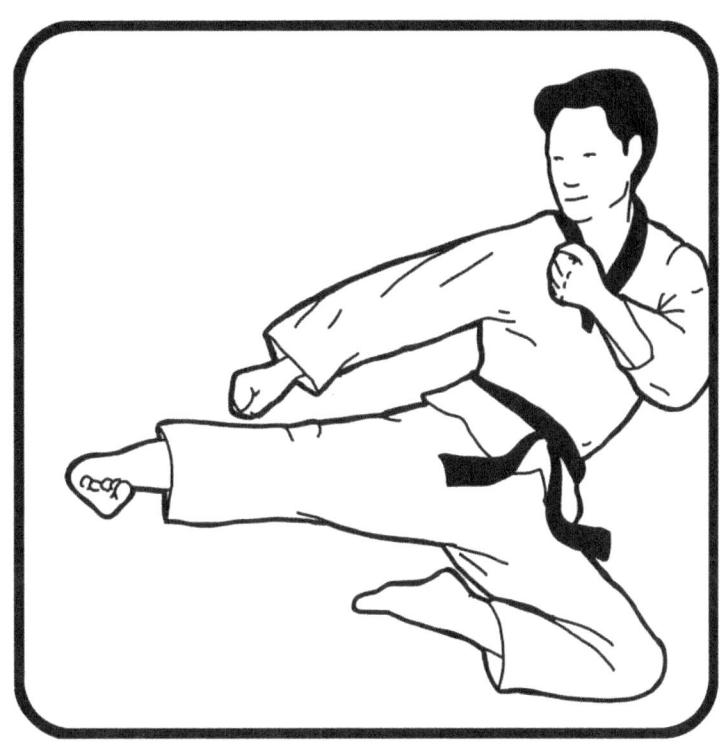

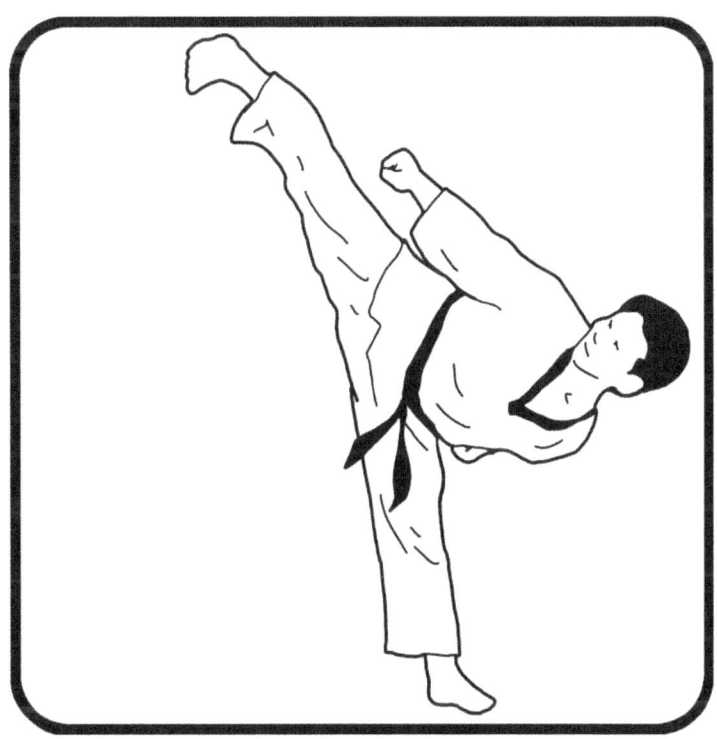

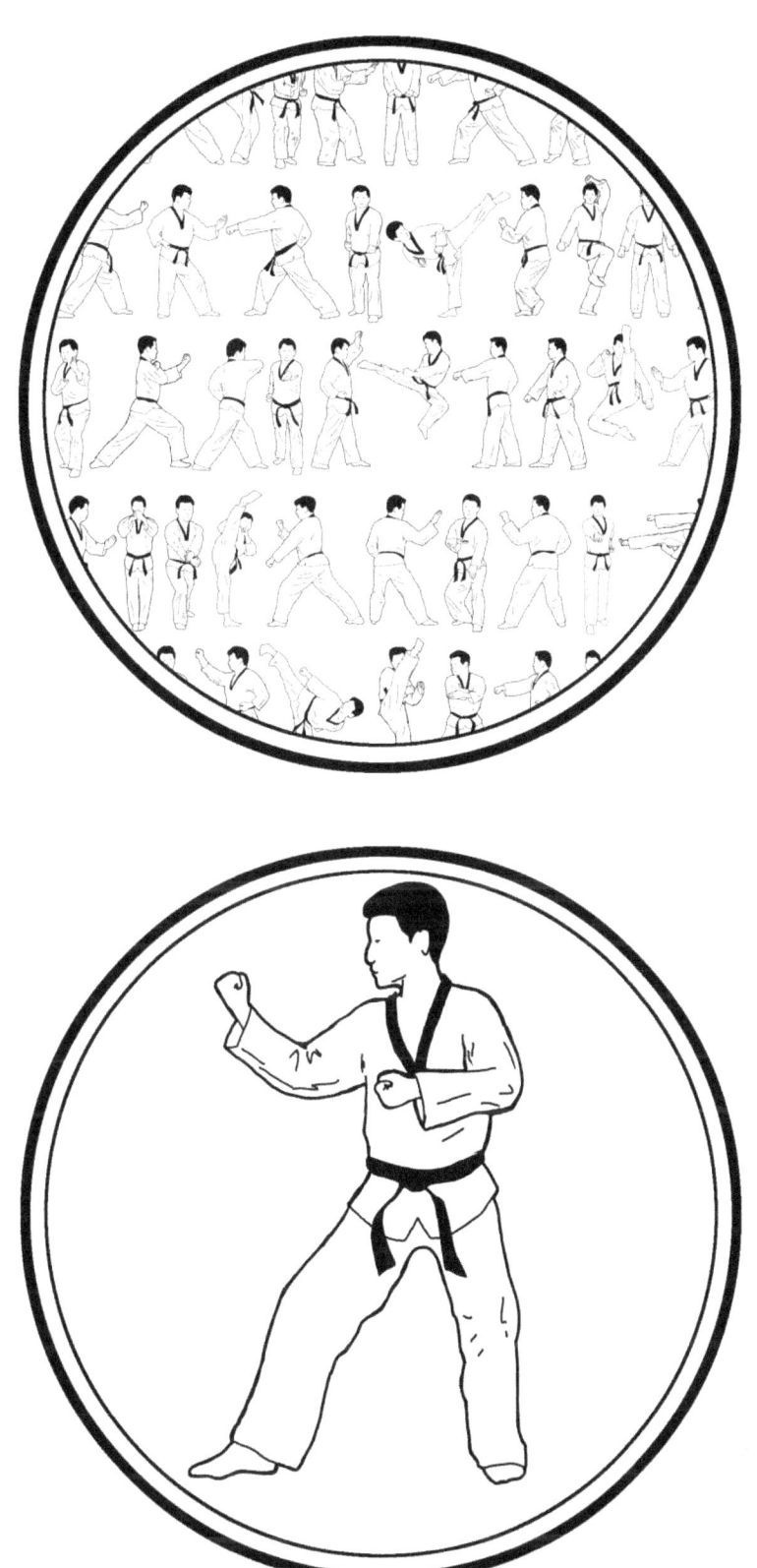

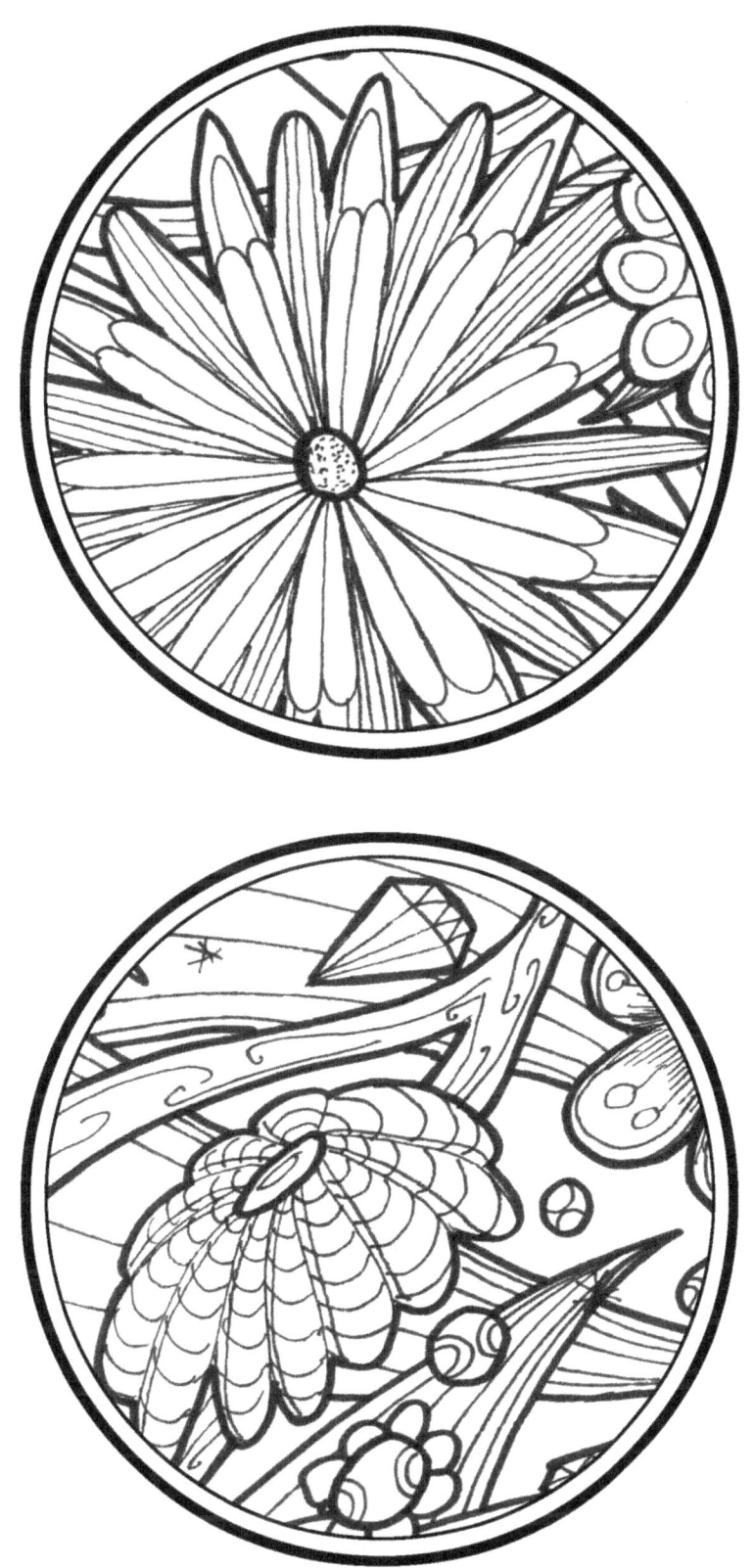

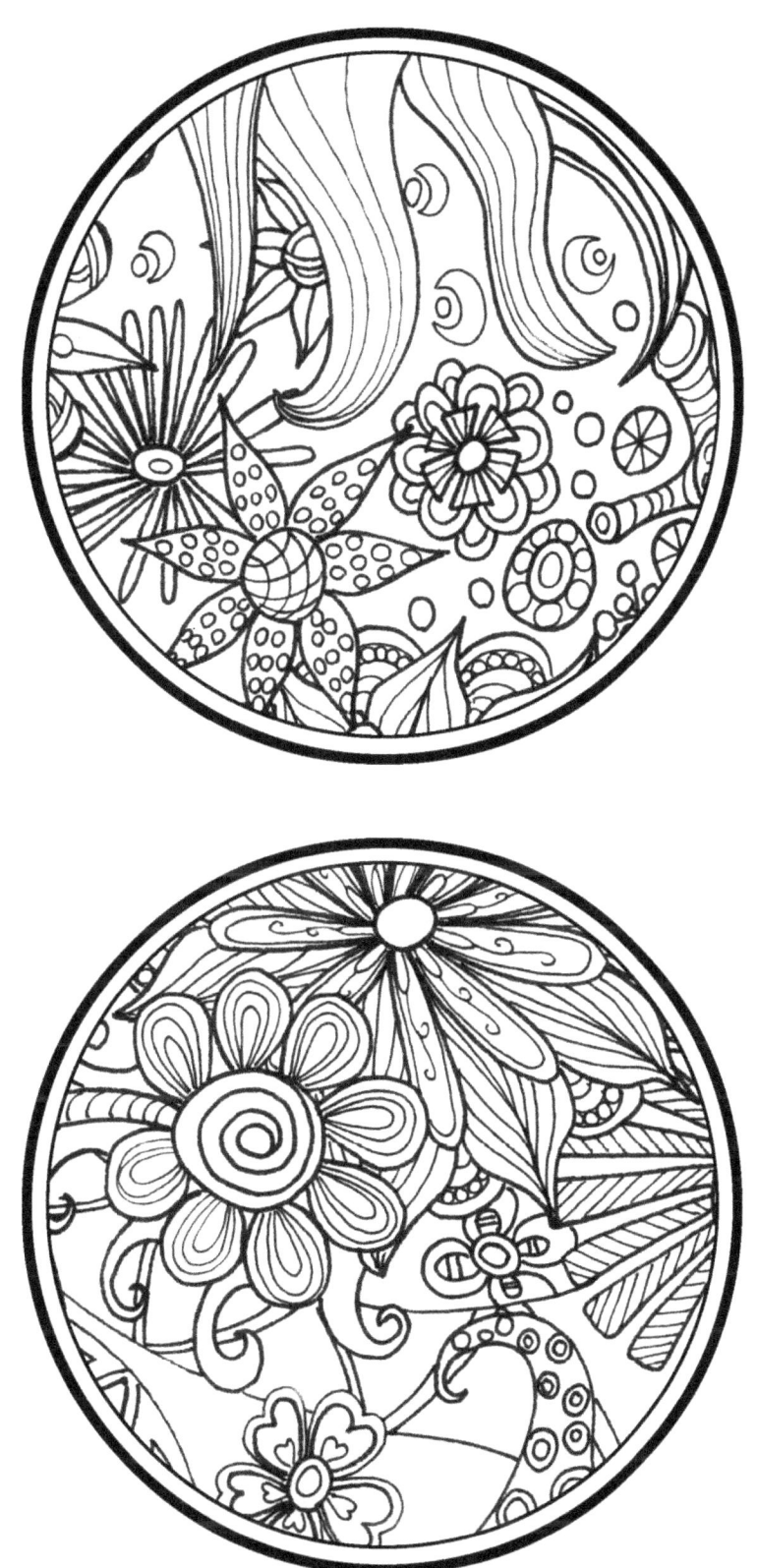

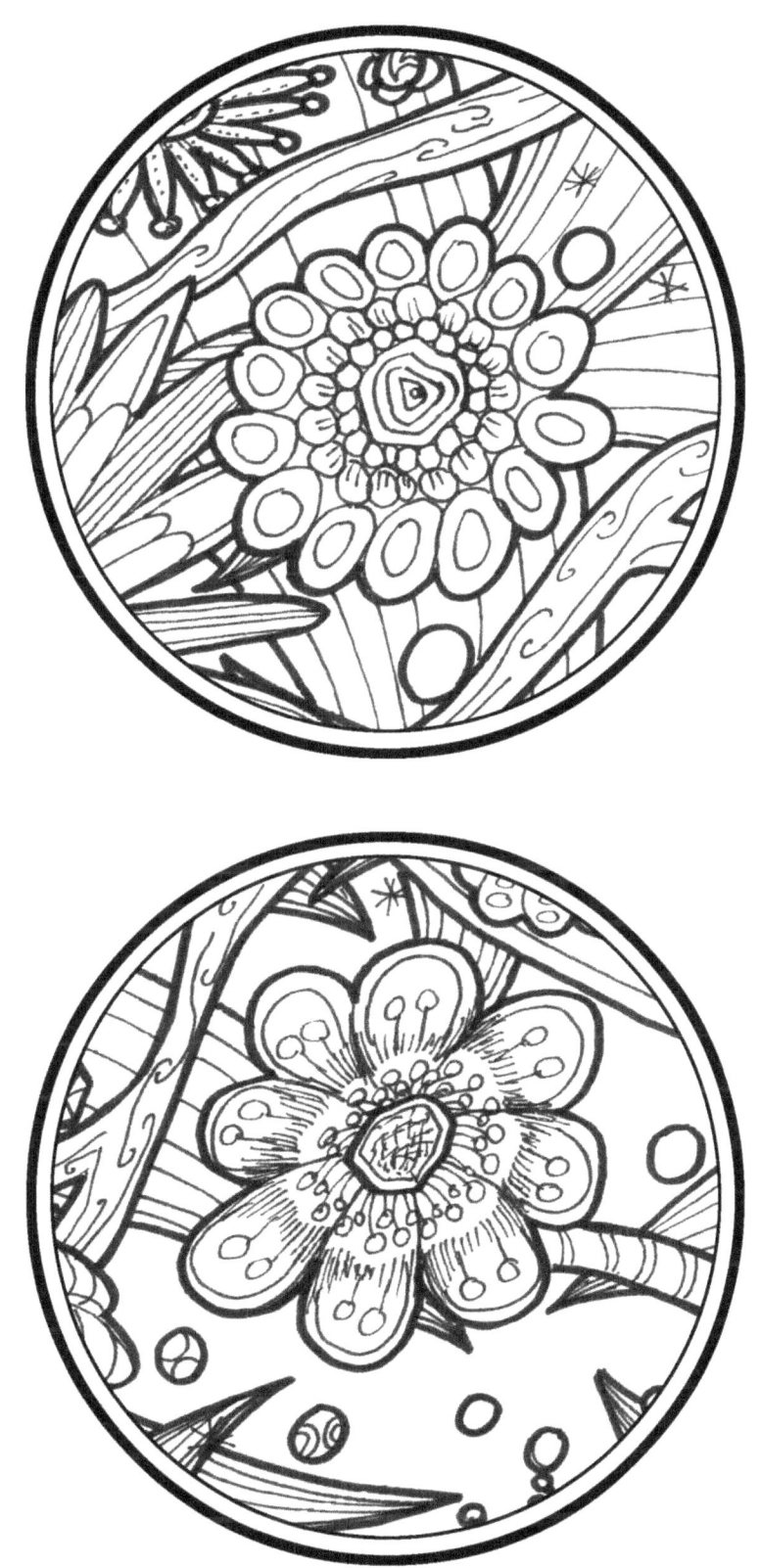

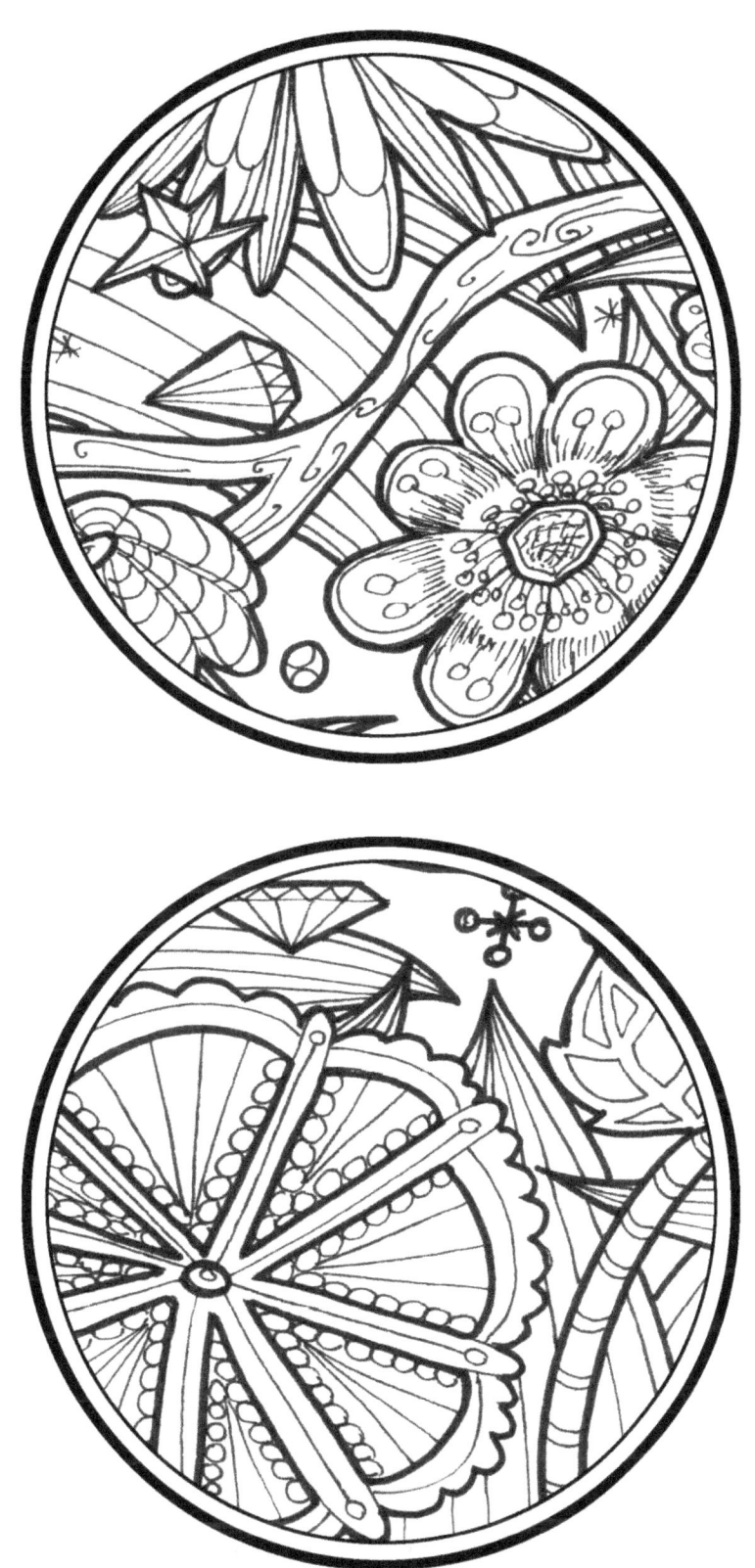

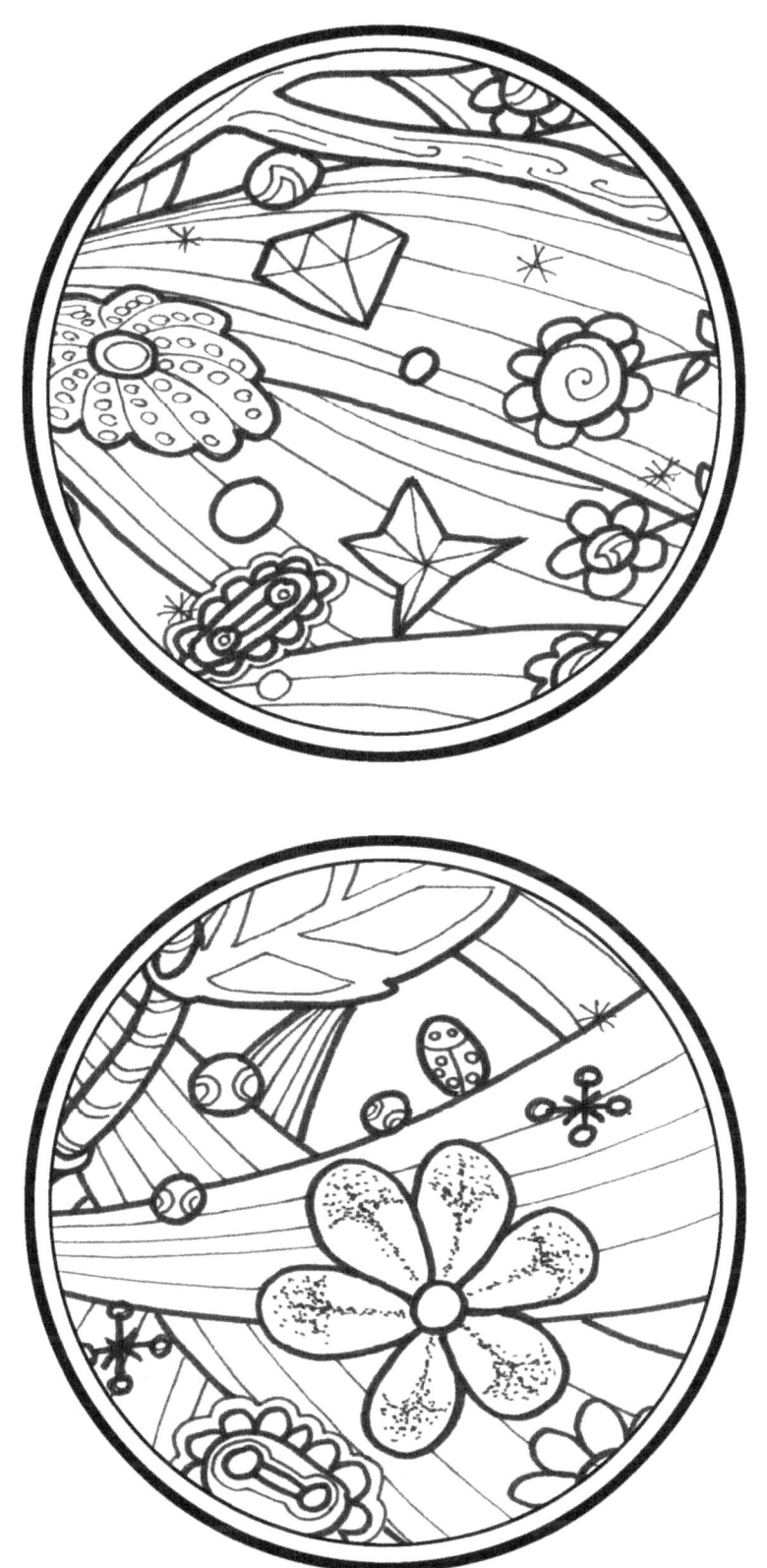

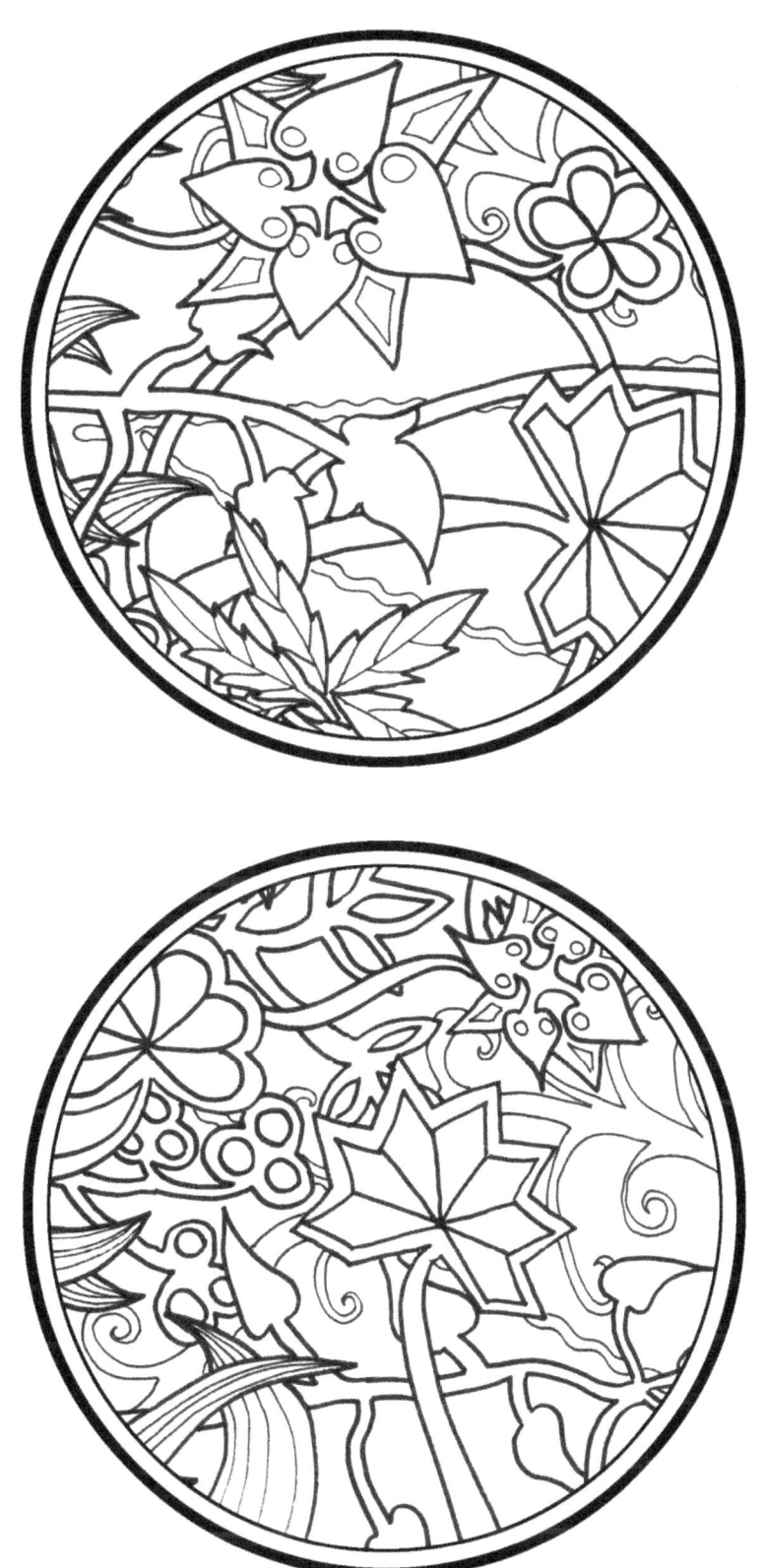

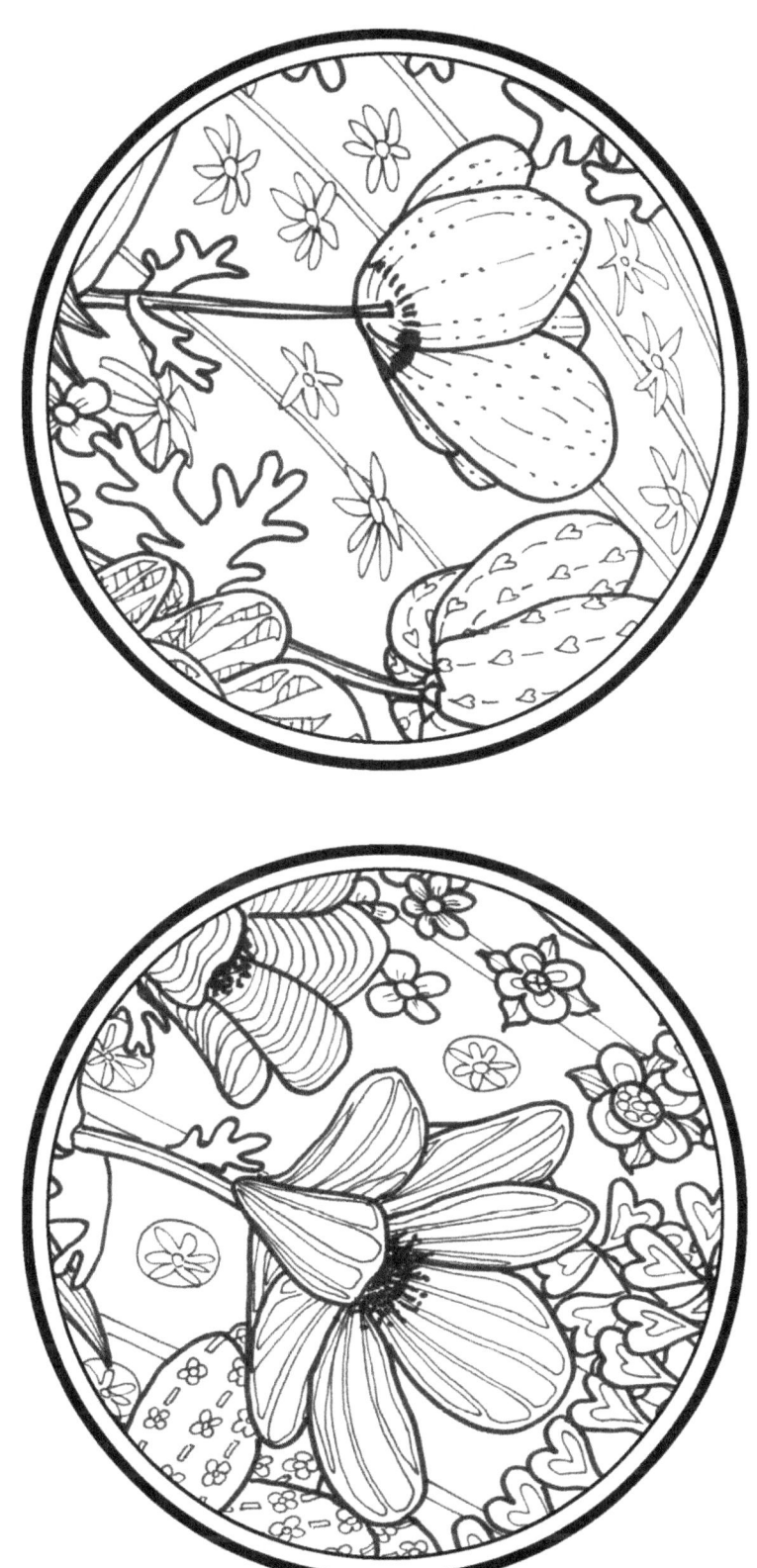

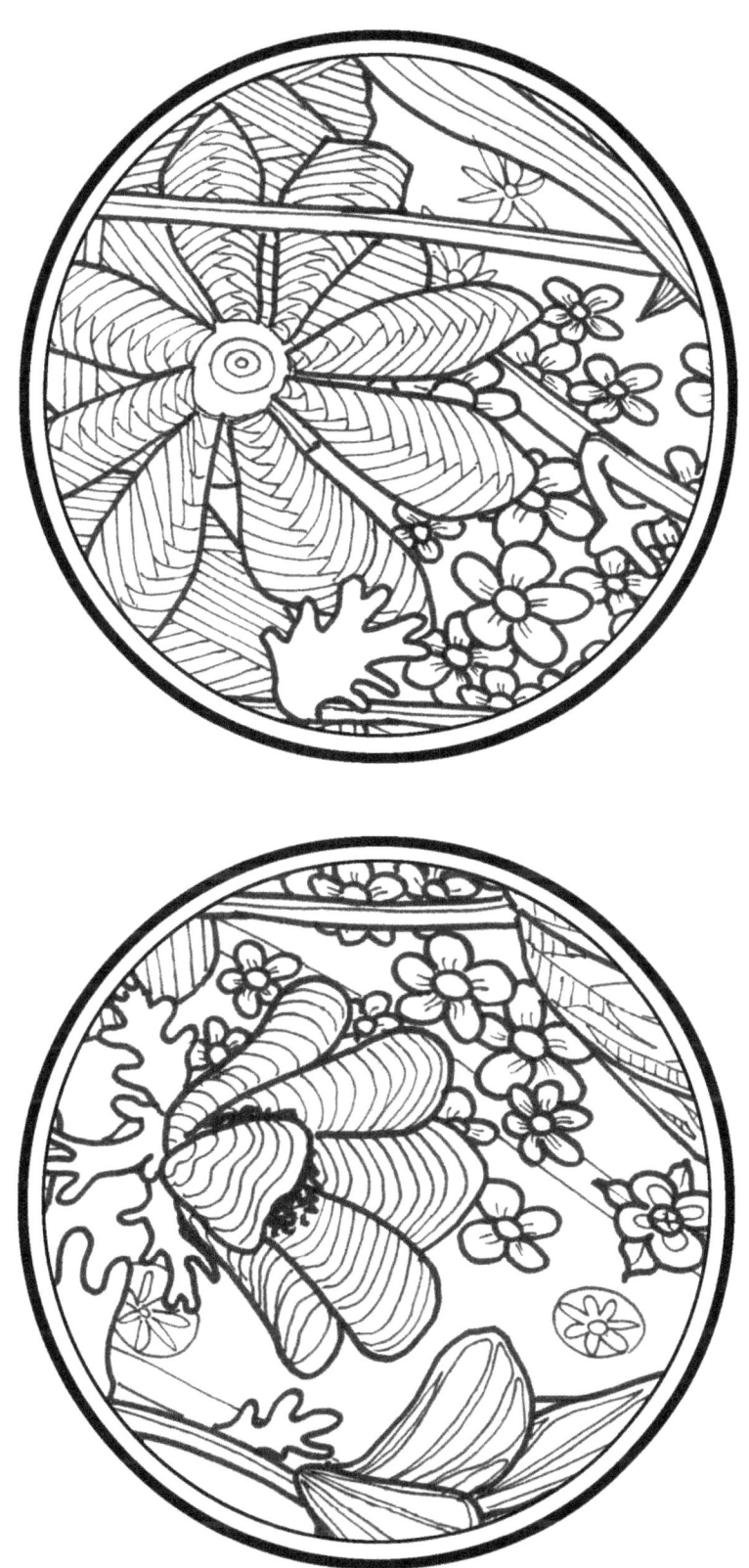

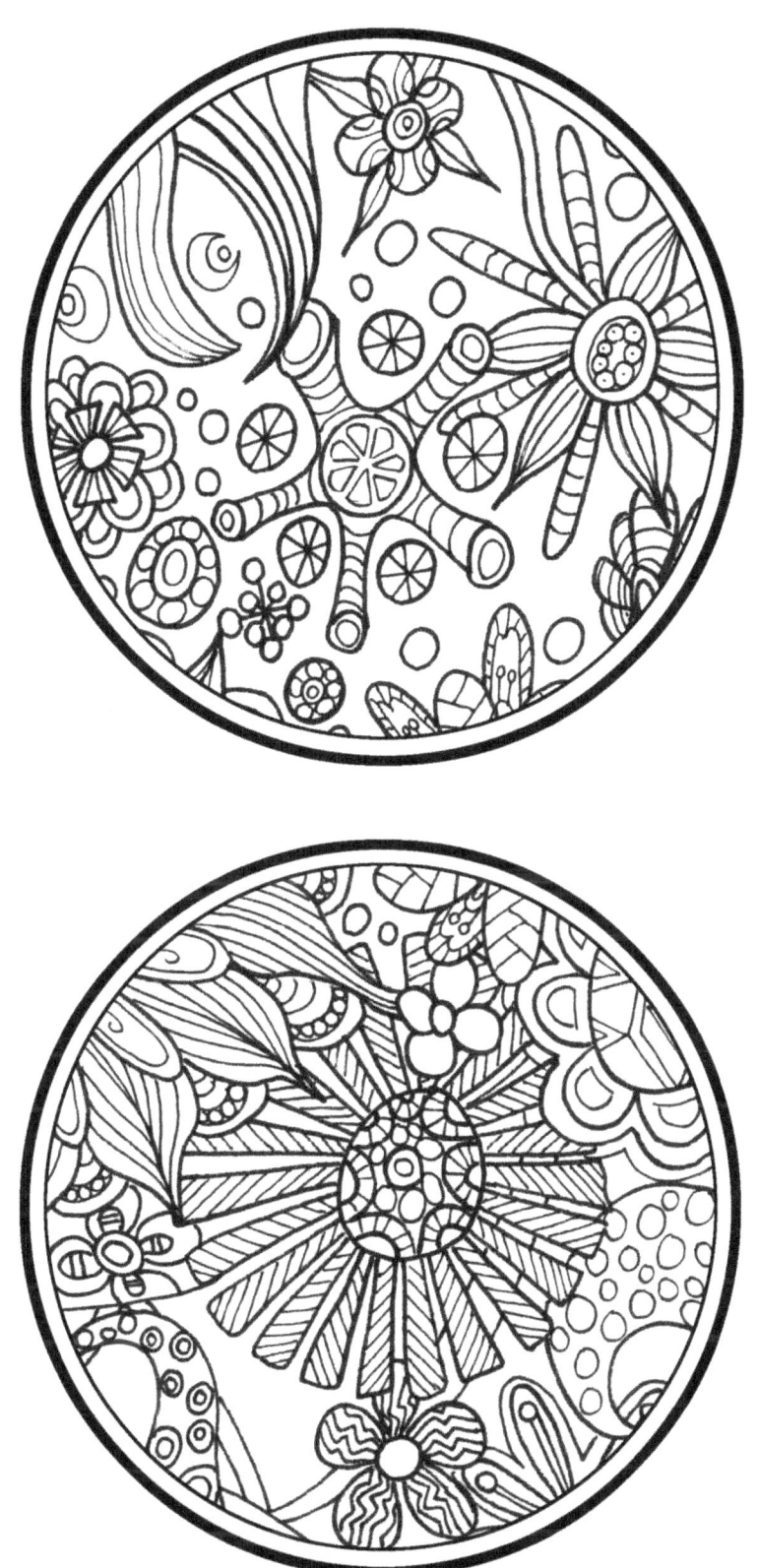

IN THIS PAGE YOU WILL FIND EMPTY COASTERS - DRAW AND COLOR YOUR OWN UNIQUE COASTERS.

IN THIS PAGE YOU WILL FIND EMPTY COASTERS - DRAW AND COLOR YOUR OWN UNIQUE COASTERS.

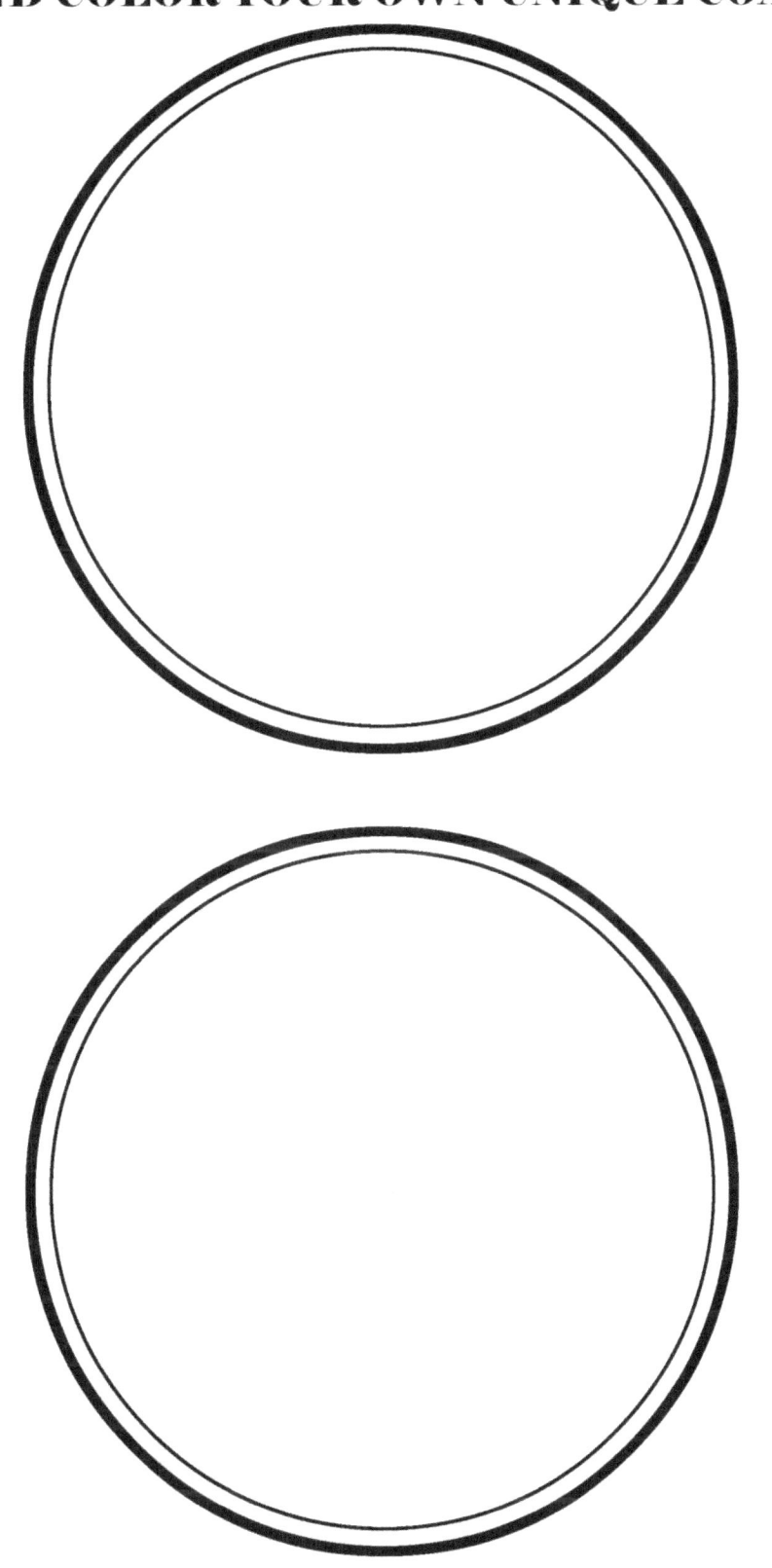

IN THIS PAGE YOU WILL FIND EMPTY COASTERS - DRAW AND COLOR YOUR OWN UNIQUE COASTERS.

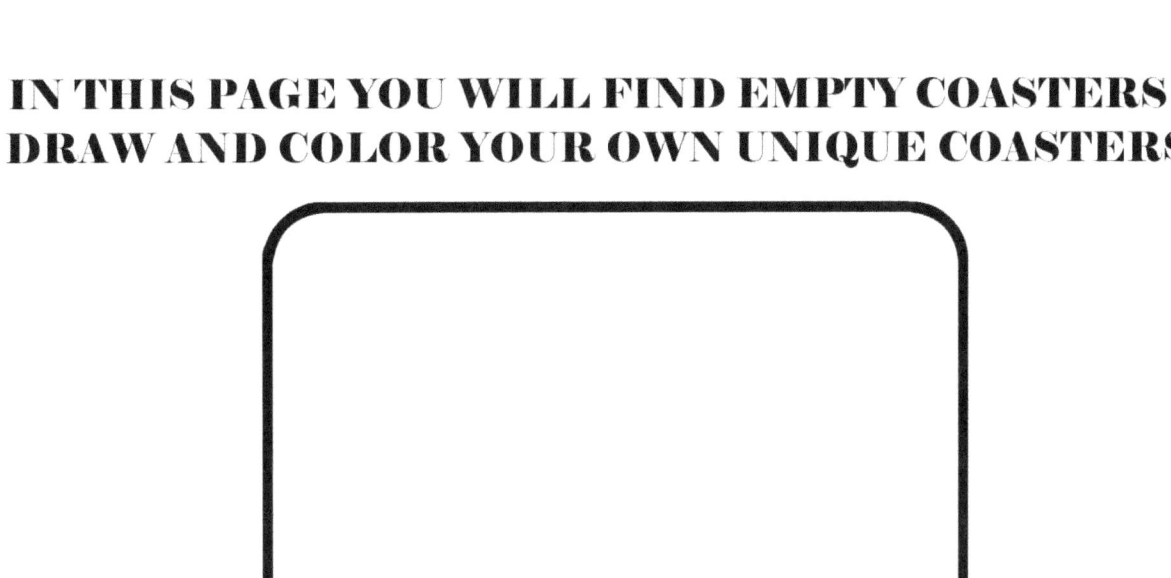

Dear reader,
Thank you so much for purchasing my book,
I hope you enjoyed it.
I will appreciate it if you can leave a review on Amazon. Hope to see you soon.
Alex

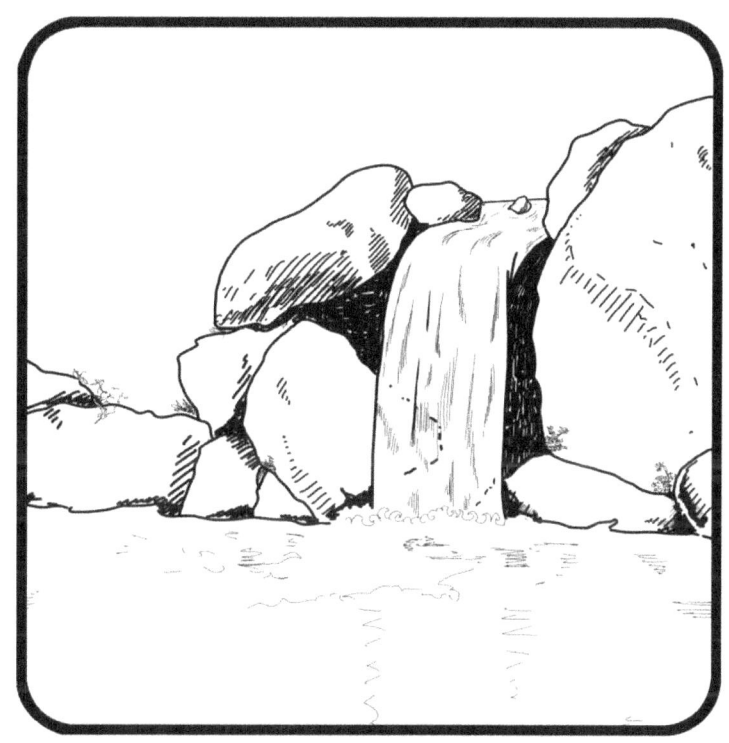

Copyright © 2018 Alex Man
All rights reserved. No part of this publication may be
reproduced, distributed, or transmitted in any form
or by any means, including photocopying, recording,
or other electronic or mechanical methods,
without the prior written permission of the author.